Breakthrough: When the Holy Spirit Moves by Ryan Stratton
Published by Ryan Stratton
www.revryanstratton.com

© 2018 Ryan Stratton

Breakthrough
When the Holy Spirit Moves

By: Ryan Stratton

I dedicate this book to my beautiful wife and children. I love you!

Table of Contents

INTRODUCTION 2

WAITING 5

THE RUSH 9

COMMUNITY 13

RISE AND WALK 17

STAND FIRM IN GRACE 21

PRAYING AS COMMUNITY 25

RECOGNITION & GENEROSITY 29

BEYOND JEALOUSY 33

FILLING POSITIONS 37

FILLED WITH THE SPIRIT......................................41

CHECKING EMOTIONS...44

KEEP MOVING FORWARD 47

NOT FOR SALE 51

HEY, WHY NOT?..55

HOLY INTERRUPTIONS 60

PEOPLE CAN CHANGE 64

BEING KNOWN 69

"IT'S NOT CLEAN!" 73

WHEN THE SPIRIT MOVES 78

CAN'T BE CONTAINED..82

SET APART 87

TAKING THE OPPORUNITY 91

CONFIDENCE IN THE CALLING 95

STRENGTH TO STAND 98

ENCOURAGED & STRENGTHENED 102

UNITED BY GRACE..106

BETWEEN TWO FRIENDS.......................................110

ALONG THE JOURNEY 114

TROUBLE AGAIN? 118

CONNECTING POINTS 122

FULLY DEVOTED...126

JUST WATCH..130

WORDS OF ENCOURAGEMENT 134

KNOWING THE ROAD AHEAD...............................139

GOD WORKING THROUGH OUR LIFE 143

IT'S ABOUT KINGDOM BUILDING 147

KEEPING CALM IN TURMOIL 151

IN THE PRESENCE OF THE KING 155

CONVINCING ARGUMENTS 159

PEACE BEYOND UNDERSTANDING 163

THE JOURNEY CONTINUES 167

IT'S NOT OVER 171

ABOUT THE AUTHOR 172

INTRODUCTION

In 2017, I decided to re-read through the Book of Acts for my personal morning devotions. These devotions have also appeared in my blog (www.revryanstratton.com). As I was praying, reading, and writing through this book, I learned once again how the power of the Holy Spirit was evident throughout.

The Book of Acts tells the historical events that shaped the early church through the powerful, dynamic movement of the Holy Spirit. This power is still available and working today all over the world.

As we encounter the movement of the Holy Spirit in our lives, we have the excellent opportunity to watch God do incredible work in and through us.

Each chapter is designed as a daily devotional. You'll have the chance to read the scripture, then the devotional each day.

I encourage you to have your Bible, pen or pencil with you as you read these devotions. At the conclusion of each chapter, there is space for you to be able to write down what you sense God speaking to you. Also feel free to write down any prayers. Use the journal as a way to record your conversations with the Living God.

I pray you, and I continue to see and experience the movement of the Holy Spirit in our lives and continue to work in the power God gives us for the transformation and redemption of the world.

Come Holy Spirit!

WAITING

Read Acts chapter 1

Imagine the scene: Jesus gives his disciples instructions about what will come next. He gets them all excited. Then he tells them to wait.

Do you like to wait? There are times I have trouble waiting for my drink at McDonald's to be poured, and I'm the one pouring it! Waiting is essential and is something that is good for us to practice.

Why should we wait? First of all, waiting and being patient prepares our heart and mind to be able to handle and appreciate what is coming. If we act too quickly, we might not allow the opportunity to sink in. We just might miss out on the benefit that will occur. Secondly, waiting just might show us a better way than we thought about before. We just might be able to see more clearly the objective in a new light, and a new path is formed because we waited.

As a disciple and follower of Jesus Christ it would be a good idea to practice the spiritual discipline of waiting through silence, solitude, maybe even work. Psalm 46:10 says to *"be still and know that I am God."* What we need to be clear on is that sometimes this involves being still and in silence, while other times it consists of continuing to do the work we have begun. That clears it up, right?

How can we know if we should be still or if we should continue working? I think it all depends on your situation. Notice Jesus told the disciples to remain in Jerusalem and wait. He did not say to stay in Jerusalem and do nothing. This is key. Even when we are waiting on God, it is more of actively waiting rather than passive waiting.

Prayer is active waiting because we are actively communicating with our God in heaven. It is not just telling God what we want from Him or want Him to do. Prayer is also actively listening to anything He says to us. If we were just to sit and do nothing, we could miss out on hearing from God.

Now, we can wait for God by continuing to do the work we were doing before. In John chapter 5, Jesus says that his Father is always working, and he is too. Most of the time when we want to know what God wants us to do, we just have to get out there and work; finding where God is working and then join Him in that work.

This week, I encourage you to ask God to show you where He is working. Ask Him to soften your heart to those around you. You just might be interrupted in your day and step into work with God and change another person's life forever...maybe the life you see changed is your own.

JOURNAL TIME! What are some things you are not wanting to wait for? Why? What do you think God may be saying to you in the process of waiting?

THE RUSH

Read Acts chapter 2:1-41.

C hris LeDoux, a rock/country artist from the early 1990's, sang a song called "Stampede." It was about cowboy driving cattle from one place to another place. All was calm at night while they were trying to rest, until...

They heard something that sounded like thunder. But when cowboys looked in the sky, there were no clouds. The sound was getting stronger, and they realized something was wrong. The cattle were stampeding! All of a sudden, the cowboys jumped up and did the work they knew they needed to do to get the cows back in order.

As I think about the day of Pentecost this year, this is an image that comes to mind. Think about being the early apostles and hearing something strange and not really knowing what it was. And then all of a sudden, you would see the work you needed to do. How do you think you would react? I would hope all of us come with expectation to have such an encounter with Jesus Christ daily that we are filled with excitement and energy for the work and day ahead.

Before Jesus went into heaven, he told his followers the mission they were to be on, *"you will be my witnesses in Jerusalem, in all Judea and Samaria, and to the end of the earth."* (Acts 1:8). After hearing this, the disciples gathered in a room to wait as Jesus instructed. When they were waiting, they were praying and listening for Jesus to speak to them again.

This is how I believe revival comes into our world. When we take the time to wait on God, instead of trying to push our agenda and "make" people come to faith through fear or any other tactic we may have; we see the Spirit move, and people make sincere professions of faith and sincerely confess and repent.

It starts with God who gives us the Holy Spirit to dwell within us. We have the opportunity to experience the grace of God living in us, changing us, making us more and more like His Son, and giving us a renewed sense of awe and joy for the work He calls us to in this life. Since God has come into our lives and awakened/revived our souls, we have the power and guidance to go into the world and work with God to bring His message so revival can take place. We get to work with God in incredible ways and watch the Holy Spirit do astonishing work in and through us.

At the end of Peter's message, we see that 3,000 people came to faith (through the conviction and working of the Holy Spirit) and were baptized. We can go into the world and expect similar responses. But, how many people turned away after hearing the sermon? How large was the crowd that day anyway? The point is that we should never be discouraged when we don't get the results we want. We should always look to see where and how God is moving and working and praise Him.

I invite you to live in such a way that the work of the Holy Spirit in your life is shown and glorified in all you say, do, and think so that people around you will be able to see and love Jesus Christ. It is all by grace God has given us the Holy Spirit. Through this grace and the life He calls us to, we get to experience a rush, a new kind of excitement and joy to share the love and grace of Jesus Christ with all we encounter.

JOURNAL TIME! How have you experienced the power of the Holy Spirit in your life? Do you think God may be leading you to be part of revival in your area? How so?

COMMUNITY

Read Acts chapter 2:42-47.

Imagine Utopia, a perfect place where there is no conflict, and everyone has what they need. Sounds like a great place? John Lennon thought of how the world would be different if we merely "imagine"[d] doing things out of love rather than doing things out of self-preservation, but doing things for the betterment of society. That song has some useful concepts in it; but it also takes away religion and faith, and when a community is living out their faith, much good does come from it.

John Wesley was a genius at placing people into small groups to help foster spiritual growth with the new converts. He did this in a way so they could worship, develop relationships, and get accountable for how their life was being lived. We see the model he used as a similar model from how the early Church took care of believers spiritual needs. This is a perfect example to show how we need each other to grow in our faith. Individuals grow more spiritually when connected into a community fostering encouragement, empowerment, and growth through God's grace.

Take some time to re-read the passage today.

*42 The believers devoted themselves to the apostles'
teaching, to the community, to their shared meals, and
to their prayers. 43 A sense of awe came over everyone.
God performed many wonders and signs through the
apostles. 44 All the believers were united and shared
everything. 45 They would sell pieces of property and
possessions and distribute the proceeds to everyone
who needed them. 46 Every day, they met together in
the temple and ate in their homes. They shared food
with gladness and simplicity. 47 They praised God and
demonstrated God's goodness to everyone. The Lord
added daily to the community those who were being
saved. (Acts 2:42-47 CEB)*

What is one thing that stands out to you? Why? One
thing that stands out to me is "the believers devoted
themselves..." So one question that brings up for me to
ask is, "how devoted are you? How devoted am I?" This
is an important question, but we should be careful not
to think that if we do all of this "stuff" for God, then we
are right and stay in his graces and earn salvation. No.
This kind of life that is described and lived out is not to
earn grace or salvation; instead, it is a response to God's
free gift of grace.

So, as the believers devoted themselves, they took the
time to study the scriptures together, pray as a group,
be in fellowship with each other. Unity within a
community does not mean that everyone does the

same exact thing the same exact way. Unity means that we all unite for a common purpose and goal to live together peacefully.

So imagine a world where we devoted ourselves (as a response to God's grace) to the studying of scripture, meeting together (not just on Sunday mornings); how much would we see the mighty and awe-filled acts of God in our midst because we're open to them? Be prepared for the work of God in our midst and just see how people will be part of a community true to their faith and devoted to God in all aspects of their life.

What does this kind of life look like for you?

Let's pray for revival and God's presence to be known all around us, so others know and experience the Kingdom of Heaven.

JOURNAL TIME! What is your ideal of what a community does together? How is the Holy Spirit using your community for local and world transformation?

RISE AND WALK

Read Acts chapter 3.

One of the best lessons I have heard from prayer reminds us to pay attention when we are praying, especially in public. So much of the time, we tend to want to be by ourselves. We'll have our eyes closed. We'll try to keep everything quiet. But then, what if the noise is too much to turn off? What if we continue getting interrupted while we're praying?

There are times, I believe God allows interruptions during our prayer time with him because he is desiring us to connect with another person who is in need. If our prayers are communication with the Creator, should we be surprised when he is asking us to be an answer to another person's prayers?

Peter and John, in today's passage, are on their way to pray at the appointed time. They had a schedule. They had things to do. That's when they got interrupted by someone asking for help. Granted, this was someone who asks for help all the time by begging for money, for food, etc. We have seen this kind of situation in our dailylives. The same person is asking for assistance. Sometimes we give them the pocket change we have.

Sometimes we'll buy them food. But is this what they are really after?

In the short term, we are all looking for what we need at that moment. We all need food. We all need some sort of currency. But don't we need relationships even more? Don't we all have a need, deep down, to know we are valued?

As I am writing this, I am convicted. As a husband, as a father, as a pastor, I am always around people who need something from me. Can I give them everything all the time? It is challenging, and I would burn out and run out of care quickly. What I can provide more generously than anything else is a relationship.

Now, this also means that I can point them to Jesus Christ as much as possible, so they have an opportunity to experience grace, to experience his love, to experience being valued. It is through Jesus' love and mercy for me that I am able to go out and share his love with all those I come in contact with.

The apostles had three solid years with Jesus. They had a great relationship with him. It is because of that relationship they were able to go and share the good news of Life. When they came across this man who was begging for food and money, they did not really have any to spare. But they did have something precious. The gift of grace. They offered him Christ.

"Rise up and walk." Go into the world knowing you are loved by the Creator. Get up and realize you have been given gifts and talents to be part of another person's life. Rise, share God's love through acts of mercy, yes; but also through kind words. Give what you can. Rise up in the strength of Jesus Christ. Go on your way. Since he changed your life, go with him to change the world.

Rise up and walk.

JOURNAL TIME! How do you respond when you come across someone in need? Why do you think you respond this way? Could God be using you to share His grace and mercy with the people around you?

STAND FIRM IN GRACE

Read Acts chapter 4:1-22.

P eter and John have been on the move proclaiming the gospel truth of Jesus Christ. There have been many lives who have accepted the message and many more that were infuriated with the message they proclaimed. Is this something you can relate to?

How would you do if you were called in front of a ruling class and had to answer for your faith? What would be your reaction if you were told you would have to stop professing faith in Christ? The truth is, many people around the world are still facing this kind of opposition. Whenever we proclaim the truth of Christ, there will be many who are excited and experience his presence, and his grace and their life is transformed from the inside out. Still, others, when faced with the truth of Christ, get nervous and hard-hearted because their way of life is being challenged. So, the message will fall on deaf ears and hearts.

There will be times when we do need to speak up about our faith. 1 Peter 3:15 says, *"Whenever anyone asks you to speak of your hope, be ready to defend it."* So now the question becomes not "how would you react if asked to answer to your faith;" but rather, "what will you say when people ask you about your hope in Jesus Christ?" See the difference? It changes from a reaction to being confident with the message you have been entrusted with.

One thing to be sure of is making sure the message you have to tell aligns with the teachings and life of Jesus Christ. Otherwise, it is spoken without grace and causes hostility rather than allowing the Holy Spirit to bring people to faith in Christ.

The first thing we should do is be confident with the message. Your life is a message of grace when it is lived with Jesus Christ. God's grace has been given to you, so we do not have to worry or be afraid to speak. It is not about having just the right words, but instead knowing God and just speaking from your experience. All believers in Christ are called to be ministers of the gospel (1 Peter 2:9-10); and this means we have a great message to tell. We have been entrusted to share this message of grace wherever we are. God has entrusted us with an incredible message so we can be bold and be confident.

We do not do this alone. It is the Holy Spirit guiding us and giving us the words to speak when it is necessary. As stated above, as long as we intend to be authentic and have a message aligned with the teachings and life of Jesus Christ, there is a good chance the message will be heard more, especially to those who are knowingly hurting. If we merely have to tell what we know and it doesn't matter to us what the other person thinks, then we are most likely speaking from our own guidance and not really listening to the Spirit's guidance. Please let that sink in. We should always speak to exude grace, building people up and leading them to the throne of Christ, rather than tearing them down and saying what they're doing wrong (Ephesians 4:29-32).

Finally, above all, trust God. Believing in and following Christ does not make our life automatically easier; but we do have more joy, peace, and love within us. If we are led to be in a particular place or speak with a specific person, trust that the Holy Spirit is guiding and will equip you.

Now, I invite you to process this. Ask yourself these questions and speak with God about them.
- Where do I rather trust myself and what I want to do instead of leaning on the grace God has given?
- What is the story of grace God is telling through my life?
- Who do I believe God is leading me to speak with about grace and life transformation?

JOURNAL TIME! Take time to answer the questions at the end of the chapter.

PRAYING AS COMMUNITY

Read Acts chapter 4:23-37.

Peter and John have just been interrogated for their faith and belief in Jesus as the Christ, the Messiah, the Son of God. They could have quickly gone back and begun a tirade of bashing the religious leaders, but they did something different.

Instead of badmouthing, according to the scripture, they gave an account of what was said. Then the group lifted a prayer to God, as a community of believers. Individual prayers to God are powerful; but there is something incredible that occurs when we pray as a group, as a community.

Praying together in a group does not make God hear our prayer more or cause him to take action quickly because we have a group praying together. One of the most powerful things that take place is a group of people, a community, is changed in the heart. That is often more powerful than anything we desire God to do because our hearts, more times than not, are bend toward one goal, and that is not always what God is desiring from us. To break into the human heart, God patiently waits for an opening of compassion, just a chance.

This is not saying that God working in our lives is entirely dependent on us. God is already present and active in our lives. "God coming into our heart" is more of allowing ourselves to be awakened to the already present and working Holy Spirit of God that is working within us. Coming to that realization changes everything about us. Coming to that realization as a community makes great waves of revival and gives way to more people experiencing the real presence of the Kingdom of Heaven right here, right now.

What can change when we pray as a community? We understand that everything we have can and should be used in some way to benefit the lives of those around us. Think about that for a minute. Does that make sense? Shouldn't we be the ones to benefit from what we have? The answer is both "yes", and "no" answer. Yes, we benefit from what we have, AND we have the opportunity to use what we have to follow the guidance of the Holy Spirit and make an impact in another life.

I believe this is what the believers experienced. "None of them would say, "This is mine!" about any of their possessions;" but they allowed what they have been entrusted with, by God, to share his love and his grace, so no one was left out.

What do you think about all of this? What is challenging for you?

I hope you'll take time and pray with a group of people, asking God to reveal himself in your life and to guide you to where he is working so you can join him. Does this mean everything will change in the world because of your actions? It means that you and I can be instruments to show and share God's grace which makes an impact in another person's life. The entire world may not be changed that quickly, but someone's world is. And that's incredible!

JOURNAL TIME! When was the last time you prayed with fellow believers? How can you do this more often? What would you pray for?

RECOGNITION & GENEROSITY

Read Acts chapter 5:1-16.

We live in a culture that makes us desire to look good and perfect in front of others. What this means is we are going to do everything we can to hide our faults, hide our weaknesses. Why do we want to be perfect? I think our pride, our desire to be liked, and our desire to be in a relationship with others is what drives this "need."

In the passage today, Ananias and Sapphira had witnessed Barnabas sell some property, and people loved the action. Most likely, Ananias and Sapphira wanted to receive this same kind of recognition and treatment. Does this sound like any people we know today? Gaining recognition does not do any more than feeding our ego so we can think we are somebody important.

If we take some time to assess our hearts whenever we give or whenever we do good works, we can see what our real motivation. Think about this. Why do we give our old clothes and worn out items to Goodwill? Many give because they want something new and space is needed. Many offer to make it seem like they are generous.

Generosity really is not giving our left-overs but giving the best of what we have. If we were to be generous people honestly, we would give away the things (food, clothing, items, time) that we could use for our personal consumption but know that another person will benefit more.

Our desire to be recognized for giving feeds our ego and gives us pride because we are doing something to "help others." Ananias and Sapphira were in this same boat. They were trying to hide what they really had and only gave because they wanted to look good in front of the other people. They were not motivated by generosity; but, instead driven by their pride and ego. Underlying all of this is really a lack of trust that God will provide what we need, and we do not need to hold back to save for ourselves, especially if we have decided to be generous.

These are some harsh words to read in scripture. I imagine many people choose to skip this particular passage. My guess for why people would skip this passage is because it is something that God is desiring to work on in each of us and we don't feel comfortable with the Holy Spirit convicting us.

Take joy in the truth that you and I are being remade and recreated into the image God created us to be in.

Take joy when we go through inner conviction and turmoil so we can get to the place where God desires us. Take comfort in the fact that when we allow God into our lives, his Holy Spirit works within us and transforms us. It is because of this transformation that great signs and wonders will be shown through our lives.

True generosity will live. Because of the grace God has given us, we get to experience this incredible power in and through our lives and be part of the redemption of the world.

JOURNAL TIME! When have you desired recognition to boost your pride? Are you as generous as you say you are? Why or Why not? How is God working in your heart through this passage?

BEYOND JEALOUSY

Read Acts chapter 5:17-42.

J ealousy. We all get jealous at times. Sometimes we don't even want to admit we feel this emotion. Jealousy, when left unchecked, causes us to act in irrational and hurtful ways. Oh, we want to feel excitement for the accomplishments and gifts of other people; but deep down we wish it would get us that recognition so we can try to do anything to undermine the work of another.

Often times, when I write a blog about scripture, I can see my own flawed nature. This is hard because I would like to think I am always striving to encourage and develop others; but honestly, this is not always the case. My guess is this same thing happens to you, would you admit it?

So where does jealousy come from? Our flawed humanity seems to be always seeking to acquire and use what we do not have. This is why the 10th Commandment is "do not covet anything of your neighbor's." (See Exodus 20:17) Why is this included? I believe this commandment is part of the other nine because if we desire to have what our neighbors (those around us) have then, we will never be content with

33

what God has given us. We will seek to be made in the image of the other person rather than being formed and molded into the image of Jesus Christ.

Have you ever thought of that? Why would we want to be a replica of another person who is flawed and imperfect? Why wouldn't we strive to be made perfect through the grace of God working in and through us? People who are in leadership positions most certainly fall into this way of thinking and of life.

Whenever another person seems to have more success than you do, be careful not to fall into the trap of doing everything exactly the way they do. The other person has different gifts, and a different area to work in. Just because success is happening in a specific way in one area does not mean it will work in your area. Just because another company, organization, church, group has something we don't have doesn't mean we have to go out to bash it, to try and stop it, or even try to replicate exactly.

We see this behavior all over the place. Spectators who want to be coaches instead of thoroughly enjoying the nature of the game. Bystanders who want to know they are not getting what they want instead of being part of the activity, ministry, mission to serve other people. Deep down, there is a desire to be better than the person next to us.

Instead of waiting our energy tearing down another person or group because we're jealous, let's instead find a way to say "thanks" for the work they're doing, for how they are using their gifts from God, for the opportunity to work together for the common good and goal of ushering in the Kingdom of Heaven.

Let's take Gamaliel's advice to the Jewish Council speak to us today, *"Here's my recommendation in this case: Distance yourselves from these men. Let them go! If their plan or activity is of human origin, it will end in ruin. If it originates with God, you won't be able to stop them. Instead, you would actually find yourselves fighting God!"* (Acts 5:38-39a CEB)

So let's praise God for the way he works through many different people and in many different ways. Let's praise and worship God for the way he works through you and me. Let's allow more thanks and praise to flow from our lips. We have so much to give praise for because we, along with those around us, have the presence of God working in us and through us AND we get to watch his work through other people.

JOURNAL TIME! When have you experienced jealousy? How did you work through it? Was the feeling of jealousy warranted?

FILLING POSITIONS

Read Acts chapter 6:1-7

I f you have been in any position of leadership, you have heard about what aspects of the organization are missing or need to be redone. Anything that needs to be done can cause some anxiety among people because our first inclination is to fill the position quickly.

We look around us and find someone who has the know-how for what needs to be done and then try to plug them into the role of the new ministry, new event, new aspect we know needs to come to fruition.

When we act with the mentality of placing a warm body to fill the position, how long does the program or event last? How much fruit/results will be seen in the new venture?

As we look at our passage for today, look at how the early Church filled positions. Notice the apostles had people come forward with complaints, with strong suggestions about what more needs to be done. We, as leaders, are not immune to having people complain or show areas that are not at their potential. It could be straightforward for leaders to think they have to do everything and find the right people themselves. Or, if complaints are heard all the time, then our hearts could become hardened to the real need around.

The apostles could have easily ignored the situation of people not getting food because they had "more important" work to do of proclaiming the gospel, but they didn't. Instead, the apostles listened! They listened with concern for those around them. They listened with care to those who were not getting what they needed. They listened.

Then, they commissioned the Greek-speaking disciples to seek out and find the right people. I am sure they took this task very seriously. If the rightly motivated, or gifted, people were not put in the roles of care, the task would not get done in the right spirit or carried out successfully.

Look at who they chose to provide the service: "Stephen, a man endowed by the Holy Spirit with exceptional faith, Philip, Prochorus, Nicanor, Timon, Parmenas, and Nicolaus from Antioch, a convert to Judaism." They chose those who had been gifted and had the right demeanor for this vital task. They were not just putting anyone in the position.

I have read books and have listened to great leaders and they always point to finding the people with the right passion and the skills can be learned. Many people believe leaders are made and not born. I think it is a combination of both. If we can find the people with a passion for the task and a vision to accomplish it, then we will hopefully get people who will encourage and build up the community. We are born with some leadership qualities, and we can nurture and develop other attributes.

As you are searching for people to fill empty positions? Seek for passion, seek for gifted people, seek God's hand, we will be able to have the right type of person to fulfill the task at hand.

Trust that when God places a vision on your heart for a new task, activity, mission, that he will also guide you to the right type of person to aid you.

JOURNAL TIME! When have you just tried to fill a position without finding the best person? How do you seek God to show you the best person for a position? What qualities do you look for?

FILLED WITH THE SPIRIT

Read Acts chapter 6:8-15

Whenever you are out in public doing great things, doing great work, the opposition will come. How we handle this opposition is essential.

First of all, I would need to ask if we are bold enough to speak and do good works even when there is a chance for people to oppose or to speak ill? If we were honest, we would most likely not want that to happen because we would want to protect our reputation. So, then we need to ask, "what is more important: Our reputation or doing what God calls us to do?" Either way, we always have people watching whether or not we will stand our ground, or just give up when the situation becomes challenging.

Now, this is not a license to say whatever we want or do whatever we want and claim God called us to do it. Instead, we learn that when God calls us to a specific task or vocation, it is always to build up the Kingdom of Heaven and will not do anything to cause division in this incredible Kingdom.

Stephen, from our scripture, was doing great works and signs in public and speaking grace. He was filled with the Holy Spirit, and this caused an uproar with the religious leaders who were seeking to keep the status quo and their position. But God's work in us will always come out in convincing and transforming ways which people will take notice of.

Look at what's going on around you in your community. Where do you see God working? What do you notice? I hope the people of God will be revealed in such a way grace will be shown. Stephen was filled with the Spirit and was shown to be full of grace which caused his face to exude peace.

As you go out into the world, your daily life, pay attention to where God is working and join him in the task. Allow his Spirit to fill you so much that you will show how to handle opposition. The way to handle any opposition is to be filled with the Spirit of peace that comes from God. This is a sense of peace that is beyond understanding but comes out naturally when the Holy Spirit fill us.

Seek the face and peace of God in all you do and see what incredible works God will perform in and through you.

JOURNAL TIME! How do you handle opposition? How have you seen God working in and around you?

CHECKING EMOTIONS

You see and hear it all the time. Police shows and court shows are very popular with us because we like to see what will happen. Whenever we watch these shows or read about the news stories, we cannot turn our eyes and ears away because we have to know how it ends. I remember the OJ trial in the 1990s. That was a huge news story that captivated America. People still talk about it today.

As we watch or read about these stories, the question inevitably comes up, "How do you answer to these charges against you? How do you plead?" Now, we pay attention to what the person says. Our system is set up to where the defendant will either say "guilty" or "not guilty." Eventually, the final verdict and sentencing will be given.

Take some time to read through today's scripture passage.

Read Acts chapter 7:1 – 8:1

I love how Stephen does not give a direct answer. Instead, he goes on to show, using the Old Testament, Jesus Christ is the long-awaited Messiah (Savior) and how it was the religious leaders who were the "stubborn" or "stiff-necked" people.

How would you respond if someone talked to you that way, how would you react? We would be tempted to experience the same emotions. You and I would most likely get angry because another person said terrible things in front of a group of people. But, think about why you get angry.

One of the reasons we tend to get angry is because we know deep down, the person is pointing out one or more of the flaws that we try to hide because we want to appear as perfect. It is not fun to have people think of us as less than ideal. But isn't this the exact place we fully begin to experience the transforming power of God's grace? It is in the recognition and acceptance of the truth we are not perfect and need grace we actually experience grace.

If we are not careful, we will allow the emotions caused by our insecurities and our own pride to fester, and we will end up going down a path we do not need to go down.

The leaders had Stephen stoned. This may seem like the end, but Christianity spread like wildfire after this incident.

God is always working for good to be done.

JOURNAL TIME! How do you think you would have reacted in Stephen's situation? What do you think God is speaking to you through this passage today?

KEEP MOVING FORWARD

Read Acts chapter 8:1-4

The cards seem to be stacked against you. It looks like everyone is against you or making your life more difficult. We have all had those days, or even those weeks, where it seems nothing we do will improve the situation. A co-worker could have betrayed you, a spouse could have been unfaithful, people we trusted could have been found out to be frauds. Whatever the situation, or your personal experience, God is still present and active.

Right after the stoning of Stephen, the church scattered. They were nervous and scared because of the threats and harassment they were subjected to. Now, this was not harassment by governmental leaders like the Romans. This was done by the people they used to call family, by those in the same faith they grew up in.

But since the followers of Jesus said he was the Messiah and began to follow his teachings and worship him. This infuriated the religious leaders because they were losing the control over the people because of Jesus.

Isn't it interesting how people react when the power and control they had is beginning to dissolve? They will panic. They will act in ways of anger. Remember anger is a secondary emotion, meaning something else is triggering the emotion. Whenever someone loses the control they enjoyed for so long, they begin to feel scared and insecure because now what are they going to do? From this place of fear and insecurity, people lash out in anger.

Jesus came and showed people a new way of life. Well, actually, the original form of life God designed people to live. When the people heard this truth and experienced the life of Christ, they were different and had a new source of joy and peace. But in the situations of being persecuted (threatened, harassed, tortured) fear begins to creep in. So the people scattered and got away from the place so they could try to live in peace and safety.

Was God in this? Absolutely! Remember what Jesus said in Acts 1:8 *"you will be my witnesses in Jerusalem, all of Judea and Samaria, even to the ends of the earth."* Because of the harassment and persecution, they were facing, they spread out. When they spread out, they began to tell the people around them about Jesus Christ. God's Word was continuing to spread and expand!

Here in America, we Christians do not face persecution like what is seen and experienced in other countries around the world. I invite you to take some time and pray for Christians around the world. Pray for the message of Christ to be known and shown. An excellent resource to help remember to pray, and pray for a country or area each day is Operation World. (www.operationworld.org)

No matter what is going on in the world, the gospel (good news) of Jesus Christ continues to move forward. So should we.

JOURNAL TIME! What are you encouraged by? What are you challenged by? Why? What do you think God may be saying to you?

NOT FOR SALE

Read Acts chapter 8:5-25

When you go to a garage sale, one of the first questions asked is "how much is _____?" We want to know how much it is going to cost us to get what we want.

There is a sweet couple who grow produce in their garden. The husband refuses to sell it. Instead, he wants to give it away.

Many people hear about God, the good news of Jesus Christ and the new life he offers, and think, "How can I earn this?" "What do I have to pay?"

We have this mindset to wonder how much something is going to cost us and we begin to figure out if it is worth the asking price.

Here's the underlying truth about God's grace. It cost him everything. It costs us nothing. God's grace is FREE and undeserved. *"You are saved by God's grace because of your faith. This salvation is God's gift. It's not something you possessed."* (Ephesians 2:8)

In the passage in Acts today, we look at the story of Simon, the sorcerer. He sees all of the incredible acts (done by the Holy Spirit) Philip, and then the apostles Peter and John. He was so enamored at the attention they were receiving and realized he could not do what they could. He wanted what they have. So, he offered money to them to try and buy the "power" they possessed.

Think about how this can translate to us in our society today. There is a person who is peaceful and joyful in every situation. This person is one of the most respectful and respectable people in the community. They are in a position of authority and influence, and their generosity is unmatched because business has been good. Then we find out this person is a follower of Jesus Christ.

This person can easily be admired, even to the point of others wanting what they have just to be recognized as a good person. So, this person tries to find a church and begins attending. The motives for joining the church (or really any organization) are impure because the underlying thought is "this will make me a better person so I can get the same respect and attention."

God's grace does not work this way. The power of the Holy Spirit is not given because we try to purchase it. The price was paid by God on the cross of Jesus Christ. He paid the price, so we don't have to. When we take the time to follow Jesus Christ, learn about who he is in the scriptures. See how the whole revelation of God changes the world (read Genesis-Revelation). We can see the gift of grace is all because of God's great love for us and his desire for us to be in right relationship with him and with other people.

I invite you to carefully consider motivations for being part of a group, organization, even church, to see if you are part of it because you want recognition, prestige, praise, etc. If this is you, take time to repent and turn your mind and heart to the things of God. When our heart is open to living into the grace that God freely gives, our lives are transformed from the inside out, and we begin to experience life incredibly.

Or are you part of it because you sense a great desire to be genuinely molded into the image of our Creator and follow Jesus Christ with every step of our lives. If this is you, allow God to continue to keep your focus on him and his direction for your life. It will not always be easy, but real and full life is still ready to be lived in and through you.

This is something my wife and I consider daily. Some days are different than others. I'm sure yours are too.

JOURNAL TIME! How do you feel when your motives are questioned? What do you sense the Holy Spirit speaking to you through this passage today?

HEY, WHY NOT?

Read Acts chapter 8:26-40

I know you have been in this position. Suddenly you feel like you should go to a particular place, or go down a specific trail (road, path, aisle, etc.). You're not sure why it's just a feeling. You go about your business to finish what you came to do when it seems like all of a sudden someone crosses your path and in some form or another seeks your attention.

Now when this happens to me, I know I have some choices. I can look directly at the person and greet them trying to let them know how busy I am. I can pretend not to see them and just move on. Or, I can stop what I'm doing and really notice them and begin to talk. Has my day been interrupted? Yes. Does my anxiety about not finishing what I need to creep in? Yes. In the end is it worth having my day interrupted when I find out that a particular person needed to talk with me at that moment? Absolutely!

I bet this happens to us more than we realize. We can get so wrapped up in our day to day tasks and to do lists that we can forget the most important task we should do is to love and serve God which leads us to love and serve other people.

Philip was prompted by the Spirit to go down a particular road to a specific place. Take some time to re-read the scripture above. How was he inspired? It doesn't say. My personal experience is I have felt a nudging in my spirit to do something or go somewhere. I have also had people come up to me (more than one) and mention the same thing (without them knowing the others said it). I have also read scripture and have come across passages and sense God leading me to do something similar. This also happens when I read other books. The point is always to be open to, and discerning, what God is asking us to do on a daily basis.

While on the path, Philip notices an important official riding a chariot down the road and reading. He could have given a polite greeting and went on his way, but Philip listened to what the Ethiopian was reading. In my mind, when Philip heard the Ethiopian reading, he stopped in his tracks. This caused him to stop the chariot and begin the conversation with Philip.

This is a passage that comes into my mind and heart a lot. We just never know who we will run into or what God will lead us to that day; but we can go with the attitude, "hey, why not!" There are people in our paths that need our particular gifts, our particular past hurts we dealt with or are dealing with, our particular knowledge and skills to encourage, support, and build them up to become more of the person God created them to be. When our hearts are open to God, relationships become more important.

We are given opportunities to interact with other people. Sometimes we get to witness a life change. More often than not we get to people one of several people who help and we do not get to see the results.

If we are open to the leading and prompting of the Holy Spirit, we will notice people and situations and go into them knowing that God is working there and is inviting us to be part of it. We just never know what the outcome will be.

Did Philip know how his chance encounter with the Ethiopian eunuch would turn out? No. But he still listened to the Spirit, stopped and attended to the Ethiopian, and professed Christ to him. Then, almost out of nowhere, baptism was talked about, and they spotted water. The eunuch saw the water and basically said, "hey, why not?" He must have sensed that his life was changed because of what he had just heard and then decided the time was right to be baptized.

After baptizing him, Philip left. Did he get to see what happened next? No. Tradition says that the eunuch went back to Ethiopia and began to teach and proclaim the gospel of Jesus Christ, starting and forming the Christian church in Ethiopia.

Listen to the guidance of the Holy Spirit. You just never know who you will cross paths with or what will change because you accepted God's invitation to work with him.

JOURNAL TIME! When have you found yourself talking to someone just because you sensed God wanted you to? Do you stay open to the Spirit's voice, even when we are tasked with being around people we may not like?

HOLY INTERRUPTIONS

Read Acts chapter 9:1-20

We have all had those days. Days when we are so focused on completing our job that we do not pay much attention to anything else around us. It can be very easy for "workaholics" to be so engrossed in the day to day tasks and work that we may not take the time to ask, "Is this really what I need to be doing?"

The Apostle Paul had one of those days before his encounter with the risen Christ on the road to Damascus. Remember, Saul (Paul) was at Stephen's stoning and approved of his death. He was on a mission to try and destroy the lives of the followers of Jesus by seeking them out and arresting them. It appears he was so focused on the task at hand that it took something outrageous to get him to listen to the voice of Jesus and hear his message. That is what happened on his way to Damascus.

Don't we get like this too? Truthfully many people do not stop going on the path they're on until they hit a wall they can't break. Until something detrimental, destructive, or something outrageous happens, that gets their attention. Illness, news, or anything can get our attention quickly. When this happens, we hopefully pay attention and change our habits, our lives to do what needs to be done after the event.

Paul (Saul is his Jewish name) was blinded by a bright light. He was unable to see for a few days later. The light caught his attention, and Paul listened. Did he believe the words of Jesus right at first? I bet after Saul heard Jesus say who he was, Saul was terrified. He is speaking and listening to someone they had killed on a cross. That would get my attention!

Paul had a "holy interruption" in his life. This was an event that turned his life around to become the Apostle Paul that wrote most of the New Testament we have today. After his encounter with Jesus Christ, he was completely different. He wasn't focused on his work before this encounter anymore; he was wholly focused on the mission God called him to – the mission to preach to the Gentiles (non-Jewish people) about the Good News of Jesus Christ.

I have a question for each of us today. "Are we more focused and excited about the work we do to make a living for our families or the work that God is calling us to in the world?" Some people may be able to answer a simple yes because both sides of the question are aligned already. But for those who look at their work as something they do to make money, and then "try to be a good Christian," why do we live double lives like this? The energy that takes will wear us out, and we won't be able to be as effective as we need to be in either area of our lives.

Instead, I invite you to memorize this scripture and apply it to your life.
Colossians 3:17 CEB
"Whatever you do, whether in speech or action, do it all in the name of the Lord Jesus and give thanks to God the Father through him."

JOURNAL TIME! How would you respond to a "holy interruption" today? How have you seen God get your attention in the past?

PEOPLE CAN CHANGE

Read Acts chapter 9:21:31

We all, I'm sure, have known people who say they are going to change. And then they relapse into whatever they needed to stop. It breaks our heart, and we lose trust. We begin to learn that the person "cannot" change. The reality is people change when the desire for Christ and the real recognition change must occur stronger than the emotional high received from telling others they will change.

Unfortunately, most people have to hit rock bottom before a change begins. What is rock bottom? This is the place and realization they have nowhere else to go. Most of the time, my guess is, people really do want to change. It's the asking for help that leaves people in a state of embarrassment for some reason. However, when a person hits rock bottom, they know help must come.

When the Apostle Paul was on a mission to imprison the people following Jesus, he was so obsessed and addicted to capturing them and interrupting their fellowship. Can you imagine the high he must have been on? The thrill of breaking a meeting, of sending people to prison just for following Christ. This seemed to drive him.

Paul (Saul is his Jewish name, so that's what he's called in this part of Acts), knew the Torah better than most people. He knew the teachings and scriptures from what we call the Old Testament. He knew the line "love your neighbor as you love yourself." I know he understood that people were made in the image of God. But he was on a mission to stop people from following or talking about Jesus.

He hit his rock bottom when he experienced a real encounter with the risen Christ on his way to find more people. It was then his heart was opened, and the words of Jesus filled his being, so he had a greater desire to change his ways and follow Jesus then pursuing his followers.

Did people believe that he had transformed? No. Not at first. All they pictured was this man who went on rampages across the country. All they remember of this man is the hatred they felt whenever he was present. But when we spoke about the risen Christ, they noticed something different. Saul had truly changed. Now they did not accept him fully at first, but they realized he was on their side from now on.

How about you? Do you believe that people can and do change? I know I have made big mistakes. If I were to be remembered for the mistakes I have made, then I would not have been able to follow God's calling in my life. Thanks be to God people really do change.

What is sadder to me than when people, who deep down want to change, have difficulty asking for help is when people flat out refuse to want to change. There is so much more joy, peace, hope, love when we allow the risen Christ to shine and work in our life than we could have ever imagined. Our sins (things we do against God or other people with our actions/inaction, words/lack of speaking up, or even or thoughts) cause a real death. Paul wrote in Romans 6:23 *"The wages of sin is death."* We cannot keep doing only what we want or giving into our pleasures/desires without some kind of death to occur (physical, mental, emotional, relational, spiritual). But the second part of that verse is even more powerful, *"but the gift of God is eternal life in Christ Jesus our Lord."*

People can really change. I have seen it happen. I am different because of Christ. Sin does cause death; but God gives us something even better, he gives us himself. He gives us the chance to live in his presence (eternal life) here and now AND in the life to come.

Think of people you know whose lives are derailing. Pray that God might open their hearts and minds to see a better way of life. Find some books on the subject and talk with professionals who can help.

People do change. Trust that God is still working. Even though the road to recovery is challenging, it is worth it, and great good can come from it. Need an example? Just look at the life of Saul who became the Apostle Paul who wrote most of what we have in our New Testament. Changed lives change lives through the power of the Holy Spirit.

Thanks be to God.

JOURNAL TIME! Do you believe people can change? Why or Why not? How have you seen the Holy Spirit in another person's life?

BEING KNOWN

Read Acts chapter 9:32-43

What would you like to be known for? This is something I believe we all think about more than we care to admit. Now, I'm not talking about how we want to be remembered after was pass away and move on to life eternal. I'm talking about here and now. How would you like people to talk about you? To know you?

We see this all the time. People want to be known for something, so they'll start a new business, donate to charity, be active in church, write, work in specific jobs. It is important to us, at least on some level, for us to be known. We want to be the people others come to. But we should be careful too. If we are trying to be known for something, it is too easy to be jealous for what we perceive other people to have, strive to be perfect and refuse to show imperfection, work more for ourselves than for our family or improving society.

As we grow in our relationship with God through Jesus Christ and commit our work to Him, suddenly what we do have greater purpose and joy. It is incredible how God uses the work we do to bring Him glory and give us everything we need. Colossians 3:17 says, *"Whatever you do, whether in speech or action, do it all in the name of the Lord Jesus and give thanks to God the Father through him."* (CEB) and Proverbs 16:3 states, *"Commit to the Lord and your plans will succeed."* (CEB).

Continuing on with our study through the book of Acts, we come back to the Apostle Peter. Peter as committed his life to the Jesus Christ. He has committed all of his work as well. There was no separate designation because Peter knew that his entire life is better lived when it's lived with and for Jesus Christ.

Too often we miss that point. We can go on thinking and live in ways that say we are working for a purpose and what we do after work is for another purpose. To be known in our communities is to understand that everything we do is connected. For example, if at our "job" we do not smile, are not happy, undermine or talk bad about our co-workers, it will be difficult for people to believe you can do great things in your free time. On the other hand, if we work hard (whether we like our job or not), are courteous, give praise where it's due, etc., people will gravitate toward that attitude.

Peter had challenges with his pride before Jesus was crucified. But now, we come to the book of Acts and see his life radically transformed. He has a higher mission and purpose within himself, and it is played out in his everyday life. When he is around, word gets around.

Because of Peter's life, and his dedication to living his life for Christ, he has become a person known for his love of others. He has become known as a person you can trust, count on, and call to be with you in times of heartache and grief.

In the end, what is more important: having someone with you to help encourage and build you up, or having someone guide you to be able to be the materially wealthiest person out there? Often times, if we live for a greater purpose than just ourselves, we find we are more well known, and people come to Christ because of the lives we live.

Revisit the passage today and see how Peter was known in the areas he traveled. I challenge you to think about if you are known for doing good? If so, what?

Peter did not get that way overnight. He committed his life to follow Jesus Christ which led him to experience incredible joy and work he would never imagine would be possible.

JOURNAL TIME! What would you like to be known for today? How do you see God working in your life in that area?

"IT'S NOT CLEAN!"

Read Acts chapter 10

"Are these dishes clean or dirty?" This is a common question in our house. Most of the time I can answer with confidence the dishes are clean. But there are sometimes I am not sure because I don't remember running the dishwasher.

My kids are usually the ones who ask that question. Sometimes they will look to see if the "clean" light is on so they know if they could use a plate, bowl, or cup; other times, they ask as they're rinsing their dish, so they know where or not to put it in the dishwasher.

Knowing what is clean is essential so we can be healthy. But, much of the time we tend to take this kind of thinking and apply it to people as well. This is not a new mindset: who is "clean" meaning who is like me that is worthy to be around me. All throughout the history of mankind, people have fought because deep down they felt the other side with inferior to them. As I write this in the morning, I automatically think of the historic feud here in America between the Hatfields and McCoys.

Prejudices and stereotypes have been developed because we still like to be with people like us and want to think others are not worthy to be near us, or us associate with them. This way of thinking about people has caused great harm to many families and created distrust and hatred.

In the Acts passage today, a non-Jewish person (Gentile) who worshipped God has the vision to have the Apostle Peter summoned to talk with him and his family about God. At the same time this was going on (and the servant was on his way to get Peter), Peter was hungry and had his own vision prompted by the Spirit.

This is one of those famous passages people talk about a lot (in fact it is told twice in the book of Acts in two consecutive chapters, so it might be essential to pay attention to). A sheet has come down from heaven, and Peter is told to eat the animals more than once. Peter sees some animals were forbidden by the Torah to eat. I think he felt like it was a test, so he answered like a good Jewish man would by saying he would not eat the animals that are unclean.

Can you blame Peter for this? All his life he was told to stay away from certain foods and now the Spirit was telling him to eat the animals he wasn't supposed to.

Now, think about our lives today. How many of us have been told not to go around certain types of people only because of x, y, z? Often times we're told it's because we need to stay safe. We live in a world that is divided into so many levels, and many groups of people will not associate with another group because of underlying prejudices and teachings.

But God told Peter not to call the animals "unclean" after God has called them clean. Just as he awoke from the vision, there was a knock at the door. He was asked to go to Cornelius' house.

Had Peter not gone, the story would have ended there, and we would not have found out anymore. But, instead, he chose to go to see what would happen and what was going on.

Imagine how different the world would be if we all did this same thing? How much division could be brought down by just talking with the other "side."

Peter found out Cornelius and his family wanted to learn more about God. So, Peter told them much more than they anticipated. He told them about Jesus Christ, God made flesh. Lives were changed because of the willingness to break down the barrier between Jewish and Gentile people.

Jesus Christ came for all people. Every person needs to hear the gospel message of Jesus Christ. Do not be surprised if (and when) God calls you to talk with a person you don't like, flat out hate, or don't like because of other reasons. You may be the very person God is using to break down barriers to spread his message throughout the world.

We do this because we love God and have had his transforming grace change our lives. Now, we get to go into the world and work with God to transform and redeem the world and show what true love really is.

Remember these words from 1 Corinthians 13 CEB:
4 Love is patient, love is kind, it isn't jealous, it doesn't brag, it isn't arrogant, 5 it isn't rude, it doesn't seek its own advantage, it isn't irritable, it doesn't keep a record of complaints, 6 it isn't happy with injustice, but it is happy with the truth. 7 Love puts up with all things, trusts in all things, hopes for all things, endures all things.

JOURNAL TIME! Name a person or people group you do not understand or agree with. Write down how God may be changing your heart toward them.

WHEN THE SPIRIT MOVES

Read Acts chapter 11

Peter had a vision of what God considers clean. Before he had this vision about the animals on the sheet, he was still only focused on "his people." But he began to understand that God's Word is true for all people.

There is a little verse at the end of Romans chapter 2 that I do not hear many people quote. It clearly says, *"God does not have favorites."* The point is God's blessings and grace is not just for one group of people but for the whole world. Peter has just learned this and has had to gives his testimony to the other apostles who questioned his actions.

Have you had an opportunity to follow the Spirit's leading, doing the good that he was guiding you to do only to have it questioned later? Sometimes I think people question our motives for doing good works. Why would we do something if it didn't benefit us? Those who have quenched the Spirit's voice may not understand that we don't always do things to improve our reputation, or to move our status up. We talk with people, help, and go places because God's Spirit is leading us.

One thing we have to be aware of is some people will not understand why we do what we do. This is an incredible opportunity to share grace, to tell the good news of Jesus Christ. Wherever we go, people need to hear about Christ so they can understand they are truly free because Christ has defeated and broken the chains of sin and death forever.

When we allow ourselves to be filled with the joy and grace the Spirit gives, people see there is something different about us. They want to know why you can handle tragic situations with calmness. They want to know how you can remain hopeful and peaceful when a family member is on their death bed. They want to know what the source of all this is.

Our culture has gotten to be more interested in finding the answers to how to "fix" their life through books, thinking all they have to do is read, and their problems will go away. But we know that the answer to life is Christ. He is the source of our joy, strength, peace.

Knowing and living in that truth will cause people to notice you follow Jesus Christ in your life. What a joy it is to be called "Christian" meaning "little Christ." Every time we step out and do something others may not understand, we are following the Spirit's movement, truthfully going where Christ is working, and being his hands and feet in the world.

The Spirit will lead and guide us to do what we may not do if it was left to us. It is much easier to remain comfortable than to go where the hurt and pain is in the world. But, when we trust the prompting of the Spirit, we get to watch incredible things happen, incredible things change and see the mighty works of God in the world and in the lives of those people the Spirit sent us to.

What great a blessing is it to be joined with God to go into the world to work for redemption, reconciliation, to make disciples of Jesus Christ, and to witness how God is changing the world one step at a time.

JOURNAL TIME! Think back to yesterday. How is God continuing to shape your heart to be a witness for Christ in your community? In the world?

CAN'T BE CONTAINED

Read Acts chapter 12

Being told to keep quiet when you know the truth should be spoken is challenging. Being told not to do anything you think is right is challenging. For some, it is more important not to ruffle feathers or to disturb the status quo or cause a disturbance in the force. But always remember the truth and grace of God will continue to prevail and will not be held back.

In Acts 12, we read about Herod trying to please the crowd. He was violent with anyone who was affiliated with the church (those who followed Jesus Christ). In fact, he had the Apostle James killed by the sword. Herold saw how much this pleased the Jews, so he had Peter arrested too.

Why would Herod be so angry with followers of Christ and do what he could to please the Jews? His control over the region would be lost and severely threatened if more of the citizens believed in and followed Jesus Christ. This is a scary place to be whenever you are used to having control. Isn't it amazing how much emphasis on our identity is based upon what we do and what we can control?

To keep his sense of running the region, Herod was doing everything he could to stop the people from following another. His actions would have instilled fear in the people who witnessed his actions. It is human nature to go into a mindset of self-preservation. So acting pleased, even if you weren't would have been the thing to do. Also, there would have been religious authorities, of the day, most likely pressuring people to not go against Herod.

The citizens saw that Peter was arrested. In the community, he would have been the one seen as the leader so some may have thought this business of following Jesus was over. But...You cannot contain nor stop what God is doing.

Peter was released, at night, by an angel of the Lord. No one saw him leave. What Herod tried to contain and squish, God released. Is there anything inside you that is "imprisoned" that needs to be released? I am talking about having a fear of talking to others about Jesus, going on the "bad/rough" side of town to spread the love and grace of God through Jesus Christ, being the person willing to stand up for those who have no one?

The power of God's grace can open up doors and cross boundaries we may feel it's difficult to cross. When we recognize that God is the Creator and is already present, we also should understand there is nothing that humans can do to stop the power of grace.

Yes, fear does keep people laying low and not doing anything; but if we allow ourselves to live into the joy, hope, love, peace, power that God has given us, there is nothing anyone can do.

1 Timothy 2:7 CEB *"God didn't give us a spirit that is timid but one that is powerful, loving, and self-controlled."*

Romans 8:26-39 CEB *"26 In the same way, the Spirit comes to help our weakness. We don't know what we should pray, but the Spirit himself pleads our case with unexpressed groans.27 The one who searches hearts knows how the Spirit thinks, because he pleads for the saints, consistent with God's will. 28 We know that God works all things together for good for the ones who love God, for those who are called according to his purpose. 29 We know this because God knew them in advance, and he decided in advance that they would be conformed to the image of his Son. That way his Son would be the first of many brothers and sisters. 30 Those who God decided in advance would be conformed to his Son, he also called. Those whom he called, he also made righteous. Those whom he made righteous, he also glorified. 31 So what are we going to say about these things? If God is for us, who is against us? 32 He didn't spare his own Son but gave him up for us all. Won't he also freely give us all things with him? 33 Who will bring a charge against God's elect people? It is God who acquits them.34 Who is going to convict them? It is Christ Jesus who died, even more, who was raised, and who also is at God's right side. It is Christ Jesus who also pleads our case for us. 35 Who will separate us from Christ's love? Will we be separated by trouble, or distress, or harassment, or famine, or nakedness, or danger, or sword? 36 As it is written, We are being put to death all day long for your sake. We are treated like sheep for slaughter. 37 But in all these things we win a sweeping victory through the one who loved us.38 I'm convinced that nothing can separate us from God's love in Christ Jesus our Lord: not death or life, not angels or rulers, not present things or future things, not powers 39 or height or depth, or any other thing that is created."*

JOURNAL TIME! Is there anything God has given you a passion for that either you or another person is holding you back from following through?

SET APART

Read Acts chapter 13:1-12

Everything is going great! You have just been called and set apart for a particular task, a critical mission. You are excited! People have been praying over you and are sending you out to do the work they know you can do. God is with you.

As you go on your way, you are thinking of all the things you want to do or say. You take time each day to praise God and to connect with Him. You enter the town or place you were sent to with excitement. But then...someone begins to oppose you and the mission you're on. It's like they are trying to wage war with God by attempting to dismantle your mission.

Let's just face it. We have all had times like this in our life. We can be so on fire for the mission we are faced with that when someone begins to challenge or oppose us, it stings and can be discouraging when you're there to share the good news of Jesus Christ. "Who would not want to hear this message?" you might think. But people can be stuck in their old ways of thinking and their way of life.

Look at what's happening in this passage today in Acts 13. Paul and Barnabas are traveling, after being commissioned by the church to go out, and they run into opposition from a sorcerer named Bar-Jesus. He was trying to lead the governor of the city away from Paul and Barnabas. Why? Maybe he felt like he would not have control over the governor anymore. Or his place of power would go away if Jesus' name and message were spread. So, maybe he was acting out of fear.

This happens all the time. When people are used to being in a particular position of power and control, it is easy to lash out and to try to stop the gospel of Jesus Christ shining bright. But, we have been tasked to go with God to shine the light in the dark places. We get to be people who show and share grace. Living this life may not always be easy, but we can be encouraged that when we follow God's call and God's steps, His plans and purposes will prevail.

This week, I invite you to look around. Where do you sense God is working around you? Look at the news, can you see God working and inviting people to join Him to redeem the brokenness that is around us? Anywhere there appears to be a backlash to the gospel, trust that God is on the move and is doing incredible work.

Remember the words of Jesus we read in John 16, *"I've said these things to you so that you will have peace in me. In the world you have distress. But be encouraged! I have conquered the world."* (John 16:33 CEB)

JOURNAL TIME! What does being "set apart" mean to you? How do you go about fulfilling your calling from God?

TAKING THE OPPORUNITY

Read Acts chapter 13:13-52

What is something you feel people need to hear? When we have something to say, do we always speak up? Or do we shy away? Sometimes we take the chances and sometimes we don't.

Paul and Barnabas were traveling and entered the synagogue. The leader was reading from the Law and the Prophets. Notice this is a time of hearing scripture, learning, and worshipping as a community. Gathering together was and still is essential in our faith development.

After the reading of the scripture, the leader asked the crowd (congregation) if anyone would like to speak and give a sermon. I know of many people who would stand up to speak at every opportunity, mainly to speak to their own agenda. We hear propagandas all the time. A person or group just want to talk to "make sure" everyone hears what they want to say. Notice the key word there, "want."

If there is something from the Holy Spirit, in my experience, we see how the community is build up, how God's Kingdom is expressed and experienced, and how much it weighs on our hearts and spirits until we speak or act. I think Paul had something like this kind of desire everywhere he went. His only agenda was to speak and proclaim the gospel of Jesus Christ. All he needed was an opportunity to speak.

When the opportunity arose at the synagogue, he took it and captured the congregation's attention with his knowledge of the scriptures and his passion. There is a difference when people tell what's in the scriptures versus passionately speaking about what's in the scriptures. One has an agenda to hold people down. The other has a plan to lift up Christ and to build the community.

Paul intends to build the community. He walked through the, what we call, Old Testament and showed how everything pointed to and led to Jesus Christ. This is an excellent recap of the Old Testament story through the Gospels. (Another place to find a recap of the Old Testament is in Acts 7.)

Paul spoke with such passion and authority that people believed the message and wanted to learn more. There were also people who were upset and angry about the message of Christ that they just wanted Paul and Barnabas to leave. People will respond to grace when we proclaim and take opportunities to speak about Christ, the Holy Spirit will use the message to fill the hearts of those who are indeed hearing.

Remember that when we have an opportunity to speak about grace, take it. You never know how the Holy Spirit will be experienced in the hearts of the people listening. Let's continually work to build people up and bring the Kingdom of God with us wherever we are.

JOURNAL TIME! Do you take every opportunity to proclaim Jesus Christ? Why or Why not?

CONFIDENCE IN THE CALLING

Read Acts chapter 14:1-7

It's the same things that have happened to Paul and Barnabas before. People are undermining the truths they are speaking and are doing everything they can to discredit and remove the "threat" other leaders consider Paul to be. Have you experienced this kind of situation in your life?

Being a leader is difficult. It is a calling. It is a lifestyle. It is who God created the leader to be. Leadership is challenging and not for the faint-hearted. Please don't let this discourage you. Being a leader is also very rewarding. People in leadership, who exercise their gifts effectively, motivate and encourage others to reach toward a higher standard of living. When a leader answers the call of God in their lives, guiding people to see the work of the Living God all around is an incredible experience.

The thing I see, in this passage today, is how Paul and Barnabas kept growing in their confidence of being God's servants because they paid more attention to the results than to the hardships that were going on around them and to them. Did you notice that people kept responding to the grace of God? Even in the midst of difficulty, the middle of tragedy, chaos, God's shining light came through, and people's lives are changed because of the work of the Holy Spirit.

Look around you, what do you see? Do you see more of the good or the bad around you? When you wake up each morning, what do you look forward to each day? I would encourage you to find ways to start each day by praising God for all the ways He is working in the world.

Now, this does not mean all we need to do is change our attitudes. This means we do change our minds, we change our hearts. Change happens with the work of the Holy Spirit is your life. It is not something we can do on our own. This change, this renewing of our hearts and minds happens when we are open to the Spirit working in us and allowing our eyes to see the incredible things that are really going on around us.

As you pay attention to the work of Jesus Christ, you have many chances to remember Who called you, and Who continues to work in and through you. I pray you grow in your confidence in Christ. Remember it is through Christ we get the power, direction, grace, and determination to do the work He calls people to do.

Stay confident with Christ's work in you and around you. As you stay confident in Christ's work, I hope you can remain confident in the work Christ called you to do.

JOURNAL TIME! How do you maintain confidence in the work God has called you to?

STRENGTH TO STAND

Read Acts chapter 14:8-20

The passage today has many things going on. First of all, we see Paul and Barnabas come upon a man who was crippled in his legs and couldn't walk. Paul heals the man who is able to walk. The people in the crowd see the miracle and call Paul and Barnabas gods. Paul gets stoned. All in a day's work, right?

For Paul this basically was normal, it seems. Every time he went to a new place, the people would either love him, making him as high as a god, or despising him, forcing him to leave, either on his own or by stoning/lashing him. Sounds like a cool job, doesn't it?

But pay attention to what is happening here in this passage. Paul and Barnabas come upon a man who couldn't walk. Now we, in our cities and day to day life, see people all the time who seemingly cannot take care of themselves. Most of the time, people just walk on past. After all, "God helps those who help themselves," right? Nope. God uses people to help those who cannot help themselves. Paul goes beyond any prejudice for a begging man, and (with the power of the Holy Spirit) heals him. The man is now able to walk and live his life all because someone stopped and gave him what he needed: physical healing which could have led to his spiritual healing.

The crowd seeing all of this happen, think that Paul and Barnabas have special powers and begin to elevate them into the position of their gods. Paul began to teach the people where the real power comes from and how the man was able to be healed and who the real God is.

After hearing about the one true God, people in the crowd became angry. Makes sense. You don't like people flat out telling you you're wrong. Pride becomes an issue here. People in the crowd did not want anyone to "mess with" their beliefs, so they stoned Paul.

Think about how this passage can relate to you today, this week. The man who was crippled needed someone to help him. We all need help at times and are grateful when someone pays attention and offers assistance. But this is not just about us needing help.

Paul was the person God used to heal the man. You and I get to be people God used to bring his healing power, grace, and presence wherever we are. By the grace of God, we get to be the answer to another person's prayers if we're paying attention to the voice and prompting of the Holy Spirit within us.

There will be things you and I do that people will love and want to tell us how good we are at what we do. Look how Paul turned this. He did not allow the crowd's praise to inflate his ego. He turned it back on the crowd, with humility, and told them about the real God of the universe. But, the people were threatened by an outsider coming in to tell them their whole lives were wrong.

Stand strong when someone helps. Accept the help. God may have brought them to you because of your prayers.

Stand strong with the mission that God has given you. Be an encourager, lift people up, bring the message of God's love and presence wherever you are.

Stand strong in who God says you are. The praise of people will only make us conceited; but when our faith is in God through Jesus Christ, we can keep the right perspective of who and whose we are.

Even when it hurts or you're being criticized for following Christ, stand strong that he is using you in mighty ways and trust he will continue to lead and guide you each and every day.

Stand strong.

JOURNAL TIME! How have you been able to stand strong in the face of opposition or trouble?

ENCOURAGED & STRENGTHENED

Read Acts chapter 14:21-28

Paul and Barnabas are on a mission. They have traveled many miles. They have endured hardships and harassment like not many other Christians at the time. What is impressive is how the joy of Christ has kept them moving and doing what they were called to do!

Think back for a minute about when you had to keep doing your job or any task you just had no energy to do. How easy is it to keep going when you do not feel supported, you do not feel like anything is getting done? Or How easy is it to quit altogether? We all have been in situations like this.

I am in a season of my life where my wife and I have 3 children (8, 9, & 9 months old). Day after day it seems like we are having to clean things up, fix something that broke, etc. If you have children, you will definitely understand. But, no matter how drained we are, no matter how it seems like we are just doing the same thing day after day, there is a joy and strength that comes within us to help us keep moving.

Raising children is not the same as what Paul was enduring, but I think this can give us some kind of an idea of how it is when things do not seem to be progressing at times. Around the world, people are harassed for their faith in Christ and persecuted beyond anything we can imagine. How do persecuted Christians keep going? Because of Jesus Christ.

Instead of giving up, Paul does something incredible. He encourages the people to keep doing the work they were called to do within their community. Not once did Paul try to pretend the Christian life is comfortable, or comfortable. He bluntly told them about the harsh conditions and the reality of hostility toward Jesus Christ around the world. But Paul knew as a great leader would the people needed to be encouraged.

Paul's encouragement did not come just from him and Barnabas. The encouragement came through times of prayer and laying on of hands. To sincerely encourage and strengthen people, remember to call upon Heaven to bring supernatural strength and power so those around us (including us) can "do all things by Christ who gives us strength." It is through the power, grace, and presence of God through Jesus Christ that we can do the work He is calling us to. It is not that we can do anything we want; but instead, we are strengthened to do God's work God's way.

So, be encouraged that the presence of Christ is with you. Be strengthened from heaven to continue in your calling. Be filled with peace that, even though the rest of the world says you have to act and be one way, you will become who Christ created you to be.

How can I pray for you to be encouraged and strengthened by Jesus Christ?

I'd love to hear your stories. Connect with me through www.revryanstratton.com.

JOURNAL TIME! Begin a prayer journal by writing down names of people to pray for and encourage.

UNITED BY GRACE

Read Acts chapter 15:1-35

U nless you...
Believe, belong, accept, perform, think, dress
like, etc.

We have all been part of this kind of thinking at some point in our lives. Maybe we have said this to another person to make sure they were the "right material" for the group, the club, the organization. Perhaps we have heard these stipulations given to us. What is the first thing that comes to mind when requirements are placed on others for the sake of making them conform?

Part of the reason we create these "rules" is that we are more comfortable being around people just like us. We would rather have everyone in the group agree with us. No one likes to be called out for being "wrong." (I know I don't.) But can we be missing something when we try to force people to conform to a particular way of thinking, to be a specific kind of person?

The early Church had this same kind of issue. Some people were nervous, including some of the apostles, for Gentiles (non-Jewish people) to become followers of Jesus Christ. After all, the people of the Jewish faith had to go through rigorous training, knowledge, liturgies as part of their faith. Jesus was raised as a Jewish person. So why not make everyone follow the Jewish law and then give them the opportunity to follow and believe in Jesus Christ as their Lord and Savior?

Why not? Because grace has something amazing in store for the world. I want to add, this does not mean, or say, that creating liturgies, ways of learning, or any training to deepen our faith is bad or wrong. It just means that we do not have to go through all of that BEFORE experiencing God's grace. Throughout scripture, we see the image of God reaching out to the world. God reaching out to the poor, the outcasts, the sick, the dead, the rich, everyone. He makes no qualms about the way people grew up and lived their lives. He met them exactly where they were.

Here's the kicker to all of this. Just because God meets people where they were/are in life, it doesn't mean he desires them to keep living that way. It is through His grace, His unmerited favor, that He gives us a new life, purpose, a new heart, and mind. God knows who we were created to be. As for the laws the Jewish people lived by, He did not abolish them; but God did work in the hearts of the Christian leaders, the apostles, to say no one should have any barriers to coming to faith in God through Jesus Christ.

When Jesus died on the cross, the temple curtains were torn in two, the direct path to God was now available to ALL people, not just the High Priests or the Temple Priests. This is great news! You and I get to enter into eternal life, living in the presence of God, here and now. The only barriers to not living under this grace are those we place on ourselves.

No, you and I are not good enough, nor can we do enough to earn God's grace. That is why His grace is a FREE gift to ALL people. The apostles and early church leaders learned this, and they became united with God in the sharing of His grace in a new way. We are given opportunities to experience and share His love and grace each and every day.

JOURNAL TIME! What are you encouraged by? What are you challenged by? Why? What do you think God may be saying to you?

BETWEEN TWO FRIENDS

Read Acts chapter 15:36-41

Just when everything seemed to be going well, or at
least moving in the right direction, another conflict
arises. This time it does not come to the outside
world but inside the Christian faith. The argument is
between Paul and Barnabas about whether or not John
Mark should continue to go with them.

This may not seem like that big of a deal, on the surface.
Paul was really hurt when John Mark left (deserted)
them in Pamphylia. Why did he go? Acts 13:13 says,
*"Paul and his companions sailed from Paphos to Perga
in Pamphylia. John deserted them there and returned to
Jerusalem."* We know where he went; but why did he
leave? It doesn't say. Maybe he got scared after *"Bar-
Jesus' eyes were darkened and he began to grope about
for someone to lead him around by the hand."* (Acts
13:11 CEB) John Mark would have been there when
"Empowered by the Holy Spirit, Saul, also known as
Paul, glared at Bar-Jesus and said, *"You are a deceiver
and trickster! You devil! You attack anything that is
right! Will you never stop twisting the straight ways of
the Lord into crooked paths? Listen! The Lord's power is
set against you. You will be blind for a while, unable*

even to see the daylight." (Acts 13:9-11a CEB)
Continually seeing acts like this and being there when
Paul and Barnaba were thrown in prison and treated
harshly, would make me nervous as well.

Maybe John Mark left because he needed a break. The
point is Paul felt hurt by the desertion of their
colleague. They wanted and desired him to be there
with them, and he left. He went back home to a safe,
familiar place. Paul did not want him to rejoin their
group, Barnabas wanted to give John Mark another
chance. Paul and Barnabas split ways.

This is how it seems to happen, even for us today. We
can look at this passage and say that Paul was being too
harsh and should have shown more grace. But Paul was
too hurt and had a hard time believing John Mark would
continue to stay with them even in the difficult times to
come. But did he really have to get angry over the
situation?

We should remember that anger is a secondary
emotion. This means anger is manifested because we
are hurt, tired, emotional, or a whole host of
possibilities. When someone is angry, the best thing to
do is let them calm down. Nothing productive comes to
pass when both parties are hostile and not listening.
Staying in a state of anger can, and does, ruin
relationships. So, listen to what is being said, ask
questions (without making it worse), and be patient.

Maybe going in different directions is what is needed at times. Perhaps it is easier to part company than it is to work things out and get to the heart of the matter. But maybe we can allow our pride to get in the way and miss out on even greater things if we continue to pursue tasks out of anger.

Keep in mind, we are all human beings. We all live in this fallen state of humanity. It is when we experience the Holy Spirit living and moving in our lives that we will produce the fruit of the Spirit in us. It will not always be easy; but the time it takes to develop love, joy, peace, patience, kindness, goodness, faithfulness, gentleness, self-control will eventually prove to be worth it.

Yes, we will continue to respond in anger; but I hope and pray that we can all learn to get past ourselves and really listen to the other side. Maybe, just maybe, we can all learn how to better live with each other, developing more and deeper relationships instead of having more division.

NOTE: Paul does let John Mark rejoin him later on. ☺

JOURNAL TIME! How do you deal with anger? How is God working in your life with this emotion?

ALONG THE JOURNEY

Read Acts chapter 16:1-15

Whenever we go on a journey, we like to have everything planned out and mapped out. This is so we can stay on schedule and know what it is we're getting into and will do. It is more comforting to know what exactly it is we will be doing and where we will go. But, how do you think you would do if plans changed each and every day?

I am one of those people, most of the time, who likes to know what is going on; but I am also very flexible with my plans. After all, isn't it more of an adventure if you just wait to see what happens or where you will go? Some people become anxious about not having concrete plans. Others don't really care. People will respond how they respond.

The point of all of this is not to say we all need to be more spontaneous. The point is to open our lives up even more to the working of the Holy Spirit. Keep in mind Proverbs 19:21 and Hebrews 3:15:

"Many plans are in a person's mind, but the Lord's purpose will succeed." Proverbs 19:21 CEB

"Today, if you hear his voice, do not harden your hearts"
Hebrews 3:15

What I get from scripture, especially these verses, is we should not try to be so rigid in our lives. The reality is we can miss the calling and purpose of God for us if we try to schedule everything and be unwilling to change plans. There is a great comfort knowing the presence of God is with you wherever you go.

Look at the life of Paul, especially here in Acts 16. His life was turned completely upside down after his conversion with the Risen Christ on the road to Damascus. He now only has two agenda items: 1) to know Christ and him crucified and 2) to spread the gospel message wherever he is. This is a guy that does not know where he is going to sleep at night or where he will be traveling the next day.

If we are open to the leading of the Spirit, it will be interesting, each step, to see what God has in store. Maybe you'll get a new friend (or traveling buddy). Perhaps you'll want to go to a particular place, and you sense you need to be somewhere else. Maybe you'll come across a person who leads you home, and the entire household accepts the message of Christ.

Life, in many ways, is an adventure. How the Spirit speaks to you, you'll have to pay attention to. (Through scripture, wise counsel, something you read, something you hear, a nudging of the heart, audible voice.) The point is to be open to the leading of the Spirit all along the journey of life.

JOURNAL TIME! How do you make sure you are open to the guidance and voice of the Holy Spirit? Describe a time (or times) when you have felt the Spirit's nudging.

TROUBLE AGAIN?

Read Acts chapter 16:16-40

"Paul and Silas in prison." This is the heading for this passage in my Bible. With a heading like that, someone is bound to ask, "Wait, wasn't Paul thrown in jail a couple chapters ago?" The answer would be yes!

In the book of Acts, there is a pattern: Paul goes to a town, he proclaims Jesus Christ, people get upset, Paul goes to jail/is stoned/thrown out of town. How would you like this kind of life with a pattern like this? The Christian life is supposed to be easy, right? After all, Matthew 11:28-30 CEB says, *"Come to me, all you who are struggling hard and carrying heavy loads, and I will give you rest. Put on my yoke, and learn from me. I'm gentle and humble. And you will find rest for yourselves. My yoke is easy to bear, and my burden is light."* But we miss the point if we think our life is going to be easy.

When we accept Jesus Christ and follow Him, we immediately are different from the world's viewpoint. This means we get to be the people who bring the light of Jesus Christ with us, wherever we go, to shine the light in peoples' dark lives and to show sin the Holy Spirit is convicting people of.

Paul is on his way for prayer. He is on his way to spend time with Christ and allowing him to fill Paul's spirit, mind, and heart for the task ahead. But he was interrupted. A fortune teller was there trying to tell everyone who Paul is, causing a disturbance. This happened day after day, after day. This had to be stopped. Paul commanded the spirit in her, *"In the name of Jesus Christ, I command you to leave her!"* Her "owners" did not like what happened. They lost their income.

Instead of being able to continue on with their mission, Paul and Silas were grabbed and taken before the city officials. Paul and Silas were being blamed for the disturbance within the city. We all have been through some kind of situation like this in our lives. The truth is it is so much easier to blame lack of business, or even turmoil, on another person rather than looking at the actual source. (Look at Romans 2:1-11)

Even though it may seem as though you are cut off from the world, because of a situation, the joy of Christ can be so firmly and deeply rooted in your life that it can never be taken.

May the joy of Christ continue to shine in and through your life and become so contagious that the people around you are drawn to the Spirit of Christ dwelling in you.

Philippians 4:4-7 CEB

Be glad in the Lord always! Again I say, be glad! Let your gentleness show in your treatment of all people. The Lord is near. Don't be anxious about anything; rather, bring up all of your requests to God in your prayers and petitions, along with giving thanks. Then the peace of God that exceeds all understanding will keep your hearts and minds safe in Christ Jesus.

JOURNAL TIME! What are you encouraged by? What are you challenged by? Why? What do you think God may be saying to you?

CONNECTING POINTS

Read Acts chapter 17

"All you need to do is to teach that person how to..." This sounds simple enough; but is it really that easy to get people to learn new things? Just teach them? When we show, we are connecting the person to what they have seen, what they have experienced and give it meaning.

The same thing is true when sharing our faith. If we listen to the stories of those around us, we can hear something that we can help connect them to Jesus Christ. This is what Jesus did. He would look around and see everyday objects and use them to teach about the Kingdom of Heaven. Think about your life for a moment, what part or aspect has someone employed to help you know Jesus Christ or help you deepen your faith in God through Jesus Christ?

When the Apostle Paul was traveling, his goal was to preach Christ. In 1 Corinthians 9, Paul writes, *"I have become all things to all people so I could save some by all possible means. All the things I do are for the sake of the gospel so I can be a partner with it."* He was showing that when we go to people, we find what speaks to them and go with it. He understood where he was, and knew the people's culture, so Paul spoke with them in the way they were most comfortable with, and he gave the people the gospel, the good news of Jesus Christ.

Many people turned away, but many accepted the message. I'm sure it bothered Paul when people criticized him for the message of Jesus Christ, but he stayed the course and kept preaching Christ and him crucified and raised. He may have used the language, symbols, culture of the people, but his message was always clear cut. When we speak with people, we should have this same kind of conviction.

Acts 17 gives us a time when Paul had an excellent opportunity to share his faith, and he gets ridiculed. He is placed in front of some of the smartest and brightest minds in Athens to be mocked. How would you feel if you were put in that position? Paul never waivers; he searches around and sees all of the gods the people have made. It must have been hard to try to find something to relate to Jesus Christ; but there it was, a statue to the "Unknown god."

That was his starting point. Paul used the people's own poetry, about Zeus, and gave it new meaning to point the people to the real God. Again, some accepted, some left. But, he stood firm in the gospel message, and people responded. Imagine what would have happened if Paul never spoke then? Imagine what happens when we don't take time to really connect our lives with Christ to another person, so they can experience Christ.

There are connecting points all around. Look at everything you can see, and you might be amazed at how the Holy Spirit gives new meaning to worldly objects.

JOURNAL TIME! What are some things you have used as "connecting points" to share your faith with another person?

FULLY DEVOTED

Read Acts chapter 18

There are times we can wonder if what we are doing is really making a difference. We can work so hard but still not see the results we desired to see. Or it can be another way, we can see incredible results but not see them continue.

People are funny in many ways. We like to see things change and improve, but when we notice another person having "good fortune" we tend to leave them alone and let them work, OR we can criticize them for the work they have done. It's like we [think we] want the change to occur, but then do not follow up on helping to be part of it.

The people in today's passage most likely did not want any change to happen in their community, in their city. Paul went anyway because the message of Jesus Christ needs to be proclaimed. He was "fully devoted" to his mission and would go wherever he needed to go and do whatever he needed to do. Like we said last time, Paul would be who he needed to be to save some.

Something was different about Paul this time. It appears he couldn't let the slander and the criticism go. He got angry. For an apostle who goes around proclaiming grace, he lost his temper this time. Paul is human and can only take so much. He tells the people he is innocent. Paul has done what God has led him to do. It is the people who have to answer for their actions, for their lies and slander about Paul and the ministry he was doing.

One of the reasons I love reading the Bible is how the passages, the stories written thousands of years ago, still reflect the state of humanity. If we read carefully, we can see how our world, and human thoughts and actions, are really no different from Paul's day and time. It is when we begin to think we are better than the people back then, or we try to please everyone just so conflict does not develop, that we come to a place of molding ourselves to the world instead of to the gospel of Jesus Christ.

No matter where Paul went, the Holy Spirit was with him. We can see today the Lord speaking to Paul telling him not to be afraid and to speak boldly the message he carries. This is still true for us today.

The Holy Spirit is with you. The challenge is to be the person to stand up against the status quo and to proclaim God's grace through Jesus Christ. Speak boldly, and confidently, about your faith. Devote your life entirely to helping the people around you, wherever you are, to hear the good news about Jesus Christ. It's not just what Jesus saves us from, it's what he saves us for. We are saved to be transformed by Christ, to be so full of his love and grace toward all people that we can't help sharing his message of salvation and redemption.

There are people along the way to partner with you in this task. God is with you as you, and I go out into the world proclaiming Jesus Christ. We get to be part of God's plan for redemption and restoration in the world. How cool is that?

Are you up to the challenge?

JOURNAL TIME! Take some time to consider and think through the "are you up to the challenge?" question. Write your answer down.

JUST WATCH

Read Acts chapter 19

When you walk into a room, what happens? Are you one of those people that others are drawn too? (It is okay if you say yes J) I am very confident you have been gifted and blessed with some gift that God has given you because the people around you need it. Maybe it's the gift of grace, comfort, prayer, teaching, etc. People know when you use your talents for God's Kingdom and will be drawn to you.

This is how I picture the Apostle Paul: When he goes into towns, he quickly becomes known. As we have seen from previous chapters in Acts, this is both good and bad (which actually ends up glorifying God anyway, so it is still good in some way).

Paul knows what people are attracted to. They are attracted to the gifts and graces God has given him. They are attracted, drawn, to him because he is living out God's plan for his life and using what God has given him. People are drawn to power. So, why not present and live in and with the greatest power in the universe?

In the passage today, we see Paul first starts by telling people about the Holy Spirit. The people are intrigued because they really haven't heard of the Spirit's presence in their lives. When they come to the realization they can live with the Holy Spirit of the Living God within them, they are excited, and the Spirit begins to do incredible work in and through each of them. Everywhere Paul goes, he shows and proclaims to the people about the Living Jesus Christ. The people experience astonishing life change.

Paul teaches and preaches in the synagogues and all around the towns about the Risen Christ and his gospel, life-giving message, for all people. The people are eager to listen and to learn of the One God who absolutely cares for them. This brings about change in the people's hearts and lives. This is what we should proclaim and emulate everywhere we go.

But, there are always some who are threatened by the work of the Spirit because it challenges their way of life, their income, their livelihood. This is a big deal. Whenever we bring the message of Jesus Christ to the people around us, we also disrupt the work of those who are so entrapped by worldly wealth and power. When we mess with someone's business (even if they know deep down it is not right), there are consequences. They will do what they can to get you to leave.

At this point, it seems like the same old story: Paul goes into a town, proclaims Jesus, people are changed, leaders are outraged, something happens to Paul, Paul moves on. What a life to live. But think about this: Paul was very content and joyful with his life and his work. He knew he was doing what God called him to do and that's all that mattered (read the letter to the Philippians).

Our challenge for today is to be who God called you and me to be, to do what God called you to do and really just watch. When we are obedient to the work of the Holy Spirit in our lives, it is incredible to see what change happens and see what God is doing. Yes, some people will get very upset God's Kingdom is being proclaimed; but we get to bring light into dark places and bring people with us to see what real life is...Jesus Christ.

Just watch and see everything God is doing. It is amazing!

JOURNAL TIME! How do you know when you're watching God work? What do you think about? Feel?

WORDS OF
ENCOURAGEMENT

Read Acts chapter 20

P aul had experienced incredible ministry while he
stayed in Ephesus. He also suffered hardships and
turmoil.

One of the things I love about the life of the Apostle
Paul is how, according to the scriptures, kept his joy
amidst everything he endured. Think about it. He was
jailed, beaten, harassed, plotted against, and more.
How would you feel like responding after this kind of
treatment? Paul refused to let the joy of Jesus Christ out
of his heart and life. Just read the letter to the
Philippians as a great example of the joy of Jesus and
how his life was changed entirely. We can be this way
too.

Joy. That's a word we don't always seem to understand.
Joy is more than just being happy. Joy is from deep
down in our soul. It's one of the fruits of the Spirit Paul
writes about in Galatians 5 (love, joy,...). This is able to
see and experience the Kingdom of Heaven among
everything that is going on around us. Can you grasp
how awesome that is?

Not only does Paul keep experiencing this joy, that comes from God's grace through the Holy Spirit; but he is continually working so others may know of true joy also. This can really only come into our lives after we experience the amazing grace of God through Jesus Christ.

As Paul proclaimed the gospel, he endured so much; but he keeps his focus on the one true Christ. This is what he hopes continues on, within the people, after he sails away on to his next mission.

Paul has to tell his beloved Ephesians he is going away and will not be back to see them. I'm am sure he is as heartbroken as they are. Even though he will not be with them, he encourages the people to basically stay true to the gospel message of Jesus the Christ.

Do you think you could say similar words to the people around you? Reread his speech here:
"You know how I lived among you the whole time I was with you, beginning with the first day I arrived in the province of Asia. I served the Lord with great humility and with tears in the midst of trials that came upon me because of the Jews' schemes. You know I held back nothing that would be helpful so that I could proclaim to you and teach you both publicly and privately in your homes. You know I have testified to both Jews and Greeks that they must change their hearts and lives as they turn to God and have faith in our Lord Jesus. Now,

compelled by the Spirit, I'm going to Jerusalem. I don't know what will happen to me there. What I do know is that the Holy Spirit testifies to me from city to city that prisons and troubles await me. But nothing, not even my life, is more important than my completing my mission. This is nothing other than the ministry I received from the Lord Jesus: to testify about the good news of God's grace. I know that none of you will see me again—you among whom I traveled and proclaimed the kingdom. Therefore, today I testify to you that I'm not responsible for anyone's fate. I haven't avoided proclaiming the entire plan of God to you. Watch yourselves and the whole flock, in which the Holy Spirit has placed you as supervisors, to shepherd God's church, which he obtained with the death of his own Son. I know that, after my departure, savage wolves will come in among you and won't spare the flock. Some of your own people will distort the word to lure followers after them. Stay alert! Remember that for three years I constantly and tearfully warned each one of you. I never stopped warning you! Now I entrust you to God and the message of his grace, which is able to build you up and give you an inheritance among all whom God has made holy. I haven't craved anyone's silver, gold, or clothing. You yourselves know that I have provided for my own needs and for those of my companions with my own hands. In everything, I have shown you that, by working hard, we must help the weak. In this way, we remember the Lord Jesus' words: 'It is more blessed to give than to receive.'"
(Acts 20:18b-35 CEB)

The challenge for today is to find a way to give encouragement to those around you, especially if they have wronged you in any way.

May God's Spirit of peace and joy be with you all today and each day after.

JOURNAL TIME! What are you encouraged by? What are you challenged by? Why? What do you think God may be saying to you?

KNOWING THE ROAD AHEAD

Read Acts chapter 21

Would you want to know everything that will happen to you before it occurs? If you know, good or bad, would you still want to go down that path? I'm not sure I would.

Paul has just left the Ephesians and is on his way to Jerusalem to meet with the church leaders. He has several people warn him about the danger that is ahead. Paul hears; but chooses to go anyway. He is set on going to Jerusalem. His gaze is still focused on the mission God has laid out for him.

I think we all like to be in control of every aspect of our lives. This is one reason I am grateful we do not know what tomorrow will bring us. Everything can change in a single day, and if we knew the outcome before it occurred, we would try to change it. Living each day by faith is more important. This means we are trusting in God to provide what we need and trusting in His grace instead of trying to do everything ourselves as if there was no God.

Paul knows there is danger around every corner and every town he enters. He also knows the presence of God is already there and working. He has learned how to trust in the Living Jesus Christ for his everything and is determined not to allow anyone to take that joy away from him.

I am sure because it is human nature, Paul did not forget about the warnings he was given, but he did keep turning them around so he could see how Jesus Christ would be glorified. 2 Corinthians 10:5 CEB says, *"capture every thought and make it obedient to Christ."* Paul is choosing not to live in fear. He is wanting to live in faith because he knows that the promises of God's grace are more important and more powerful than anything.

Paul does believe the people about what will happen to him when he gets to Jerusalem, but he is not outwardly concerned. This is how he is able to demonstrate living in faith and the victory of Jesus.

When you step out each day, just trust in the power and presence of God to give you the grace and strength for what's ahead. Instead of worrying about what will happen at a future date, we can be thankful the Jesus is already there.

The road ahead of us has many different situations we will go through. Every one of them gives us an opportunity to worship and glorify Jesus Christ in everything we do. How will you look at what you have to do today? Will you take the opportunity to trust in Jesus Christ to lead and guide you along the way?

JOURNAL TIME! Take time to answer the questions at the end of the chapter.

GOD WORKING THROUGH OUR LIFE

Read Acts chapter 22

Have you ever been in a place where you have to defend what you're doing? Of course you have. We all have. My kids love to give me the reasons why they're playing the way they are or why the other person is upset. We all like to find ways to defend ourselves.

The question comes into play as to why we are defending ourselves. Do we defend ourselves to make ourselves look good? Or do we defend ourselves to show how God has called us and give him the glory for all he has done through us?

Paul has now left Ephesus and was captured by the authorities. He had to give testimony as to who he is, but really he talked about how Jesus called him and how Christ has used him. Everything Paul said was pointing people to the Christ, the One who is, who was, and is to come. Notice how he also shows the people who trained him and his background. He is showing how God has worked in and through his life to bring him to the place he is now.

Now, I want you to look back on your life. Think about everything you have done. How has your past helped you to be where you are today? How has your past helped you become who you are today?

Many times, I hear people talk about how their past was not what they wanted. We can look to the past and see what we have done, or we can look back to see how God was working in and through our lives. It is here, I think of the quote, "We can complain because roses have thorns, or we can rejoice because thorns have roses."

If you have the time, think through the toughest and best parts of your life. Do you think of those times as something that could have been better? Can you think of them as something you went through to help you get to be who God has created you to be?

Paul could have been discouraged as to how his life was now going. Prison, beatings, humiliations, etc. But he was able to rejoice because he has discovered that he actually has everything he needs, and more. He has the real presence of Jesus Christ with him each and every day.

Take time to praise God for your past. Praise him for how he has brought you to this particular moment in your life. Praise him he is with you right now.

Now if you are doubting God is with you, I am inviting you to sit down and say something like, "Jesus I want to know you." Say that over and over. You never know how he will appear and make himself known to you and you can see how he has never left you. God is always working in your life, especially when we don't know it.

JOURNAL TIME! Think through this: Think about everything you have done. How has your past helped you to be where you are today? How has your past helped you become who you are today?

IT'S ABOUT KINGDOM BUILDING

Read Acts chapter 23

Paul is in a heap of trouble here. It seems the message of the gospel has touched a raw nerve with everyone he comes in contact with. Everyone, that is, except the Roman centurions watching set to watch over the apostle in chains.

In one of his letters to the Corinthian people, Paul tells them he has become all things to all people so that some may be saved. Paul is one who can learn the area, learn the people, and know what to say and how to say it to strike nerves. That is why he was able to give more defense of his work and insult the high priest (presumably not knowing who the high priest was).

The apostle is respectful of those in positions of authority, and he shows it by apologizing and revealing, through scripture, how he is supposed to behave. He is masterful at gaining the rulers' ears and attention and, at the same time, he is phenomenal at banding people together because of their hatred for him and the message of Christ he proclaims.

Several years ago, I bought the CD audio version of Dale Carnegie's famous book "How to Win Friends and Influence People." This is a book I would like to re-read again someday in the future. This is a book I would recommend to you if you haven't read it yet.

One of the concepts I derived from listening was making sure people know why you do business with them (i.e., remind them what their good at) and then ask for what you are needing. I have learned that when people know you genuinely respect, not just use flattery, you can easily "win" people over. No, this is not manipulation. This is using Ephesians 4:29 into practice and applying it to everyday people's lives.

It really is about finding the right people to talk with, to do business with, and to basically hang around that will help you get what you are needing. I know this can make it sound like this is all one sided; but it's not because the other person has a chance to build a new relationship, gain business, and live with the joy of knowing they are doing what God has called them to do. The goal is to help build society up and move it towards redemption and reconciliation with God through Jesus Christ).

Trying to influence people to change their minds is where it gets more challenging. This would mean people have to have some sort of respect for you or what you stand for. Paul was masterful at influencing people to band together against him. Did they respect Paul? I think their respect for the power of God was greater. They were terrified to listen how their lives were not meshing with the real God. The people were influenced by the fear of repentance that Paul was proclaiming.

Now it's your turn. Think about who you're influencing and how. Does your life, and your actions, work towards building people up to be who God created them to be? Remember, it's not about getting what you want; it is all about allowing the Holy Spirit into our lives to mold us into the image and likeness of God through Jesus Christ.

It's about building the Kingdom of God with God.

Ephesians 2:8-10 CEB
You are saved by God's grace because of your faith. This salvation is God's gift. It's not something you possessed. It's not something you did that you can be proud of. Instead, we are God's accomplishment, created in Christ Jesus to do good things. God planned for these good things to be the way that we live our lives.

JOURNAL TIME! How are you building people up and encouraging them so the Kingdom of Heaven is experienced by all around you?

KEEPING CALM IN TURMOIL

Read Acts chapter 24

After reading the scripture for today, do you relate to Paul in any way? After all, he had people rise up, spreading gossip, and telling the truth in a twisted way. We all would like opportunities for the complete truth to be told. We all may want for us to come out looking good in the situation.

The truth is Paul is still made to look like a troublemaker in the eyes of the accusers and the people they talk with the most. How does Paul react? We do not see him getting angry or upset. Instead, we see a person who is allowing the accusers to make their case and keep silent in the process. If he has a chance to speak, he will talk about the truth; but he stays quiet and still while they declare all of these "bad" things about him.

So, how do you think you would be in that situation? I believe most of us, at some point in our lives, go through something like this. The first thing we have to remember is not everyone is going to like us. This can be for all kinds of reasons: being hurt unintentionally or even intentionally, jealousy, and even more reasons.

The point is for us to be able to remain calm and share grace whenever we can.

Do we allow people to walk all over us and say whatever they want to? No. You will get a chance to speak the truth. We find ways to talk with the right people who will actually listen and be able to discern what's really going on. Finding peace in the situations is not always easy. It is better for an outsider to come in to examine the facts carefully.

Paul has been facing trouble similar to this his entire ministry. Jesus, our Lord, and Savior met trouble. We should not ever think that just because we follow Jesus Christ that our lives are going to be easy and perfect. What we can expect is because we follow Jesus Christ, we will face opposition because the gospel challenges the world.

Through whatever you are facing, have faced, or will face, it is essential to rely on the movement and working of the Holy Spirit in your heart and life. The Holy Spirit will guide you and give you greater comfort and peace than you could ever have imagined. Trust that this is a great blessing and reminder of God's presence in your life in the midst of strife. You just never know how God will use the situation, the people, or the people in power.

Keep these verses in mind:

Philippians 4:6-7 CEB
Don't be anxious about anything; rather, bring up all of your requests to God in your prayers and petitions, along with giving thanks. Then the peace of God that exceeds all understanding will keep your hearts and minds safe in Christ Jesus.

Proverbs 25:21-22 CEB
If your enemies are starving, feed them some bread; if they are thirsty, give them water to drink. By doing this, you will heap burning coals on their heads, and the Lord will reward you.

Colossians 3:15 CEB
The peace of Christ must control your hearts—a peace into which you were called in one body. And be thankful people.

Galatians 5:22-23 CEB
But the fruit of the Spirit is love, joy, peace, patience, kindness, goodness, faithfulness, gentleness, and self-control. There is no law against things like this.

JOURNAL TIME! What are you encouraged by? What are you challenged by? Why? What do you think God may be saying to you?

IN THE PRESENCE OF THE KING

Read Acts chapter 25

How nerve-wracking it is for people to stand in front of people of power. What do you think your real reaction would be to stand in front of a president? A king or queen? A CEO of a billion-dollar company? Your own boss who may not come around that often? I find it interesting that sometimes we will act one way until that person enters the room or we are brought before them.

The Apostle Paul knew who his only King was and is: Jesus Christ. His only goal was to serve Christ by proclaiming Christ risen from the dead. Paul knew that the people he was standing in front of were of no match to the King of kings. He only feared God.

Take time to read through the scripture today. Notice how many "important" people Paul is brought in front of. There was Festus, the angry mob, King Agrippa, Bernice, and the entourage. I wonder how many people are reading this now and wondering why I placed the angry mob as significant people?

Look at what is being done to Paul. He has been placed in front of Caesar's court and is giving his testimony and his defense to the highest court in the land. The angry crowd that is present is critical because they were the ones to bring Paul to this particular time and place. What is interesting is that even though they did not get their way (Paul being executed), they should still be considered necessary because they unknowingly followed a plan of God to take the gospel to Rome via Paul. This crowd was the loudest voice and brought a lot of attention to the imprisoned apostle.

But then we have Festus, and King Agrippa. These are people who have significant, human, power in this area. They are the ones where final decisions for the geographical area are made, and people try to appease them and flatter them just to get whatever is wanted. I think this is where most of us stand when it comes to being in the presence of power. We want to try to make them like us, so nothing terrible happens to us, and we can get the most comfortable life possible. Most of the time the people in positions of power may not see the real people because everyone will put on a front to act their best.

Paul knows something even more critical. He knows the only King to be true to is Jesus Christ. Jesus is the King of all the kings and Lord of all the lords. Paul knows that he doesn't have to be flattering to the rulers in front of him because the only ruler he answers to is Jesus Christ.

How about you? What or who makes you more nervous? I tend to think we get more nervous in the presence of humans in positions of power than we do for Jesus Christ. We tend to give more accolades to the people rather than the God of the universe. Oh, we go to worship each week; but do we worship God? Or do we really worship what we're doing? This is a tough question to consider.

As you go through your day, through your week, journey through life, remember this one thing Jesus Christ is the King of all kings and Lord of all lords. Everyone else we come in contact with is a person we either get to minister to or join in ministry with.

You have been called to be a witness to Christ to the world. You have been placed where you are "for such a time as this." The presence of the one true King is with you always.

JOURNAL TIME! What do you think about: "You have been called to be a witness to Christ to the world. You have been placed where you are 'for such a time as this.' The presence of the one true King is with you always."

CONVINCING ARGUMENTS

Read Acts chapter 26

When was the last time you tried to convince another person (not family or friend) about coming around to your way of thinking? How did it go?

I love talking with salespeople. They really know their stuff, and you can tell the ones who are passionate about their product/service. People in sales are always fun to talk with because you know their goal is to try and sell you on what they're offering; but at the same time, it is the customer who really is in control of the situation.

People are going to hear what they choose to hear. If a person is convinced they need _____ product, it is because the value of the product/service for their life was heard. On the other hand, if a salesperson offended the potential buyer, all the potential buyer will hear is how they don't like what the salesperson is saying. There is always a line to walk when trying to sell any product or service. The two things that must be demonstrated are 1) passion about the product/service and 2) knowledge about the product/service.

Look at today's passage in Acts 26. Paul gives his testimony many times and is in positions to defend himself a lot. But, is he really trying to prove himself right? No. Even though he is in custody, he is still doing his best at sharing the gospel of Jesus Christ with all he encounters. Paul is placed in front of powerful rulers that will listen to him.

All this time, we can see that Paul has had many hardships and difficulties throughout his ministry and missionary journeys; but he did not waste any opportunity. Paul was still, first and foremost, a slave (servant) of Jesus Christ and was compelled to share Christ wherever he was and with whoever would listen.

How does this go for us today? I hear many people say something like, "all my friends are Christian." To that response, I say, "well, you don't know enough people." Another thing I hear a lot is "everyone around here goes to church." Then I say, "nope."

One of the things that get in our way is our own perception of reality. All we have to do is look around and see that not everyone knows Christ. Even Jesus' own followers miss the boat at times. But it is all because of God's incredible grace that we are given chances to talk with people about Jesus Christ.

Have you noticed what happens within you when you seize the opportunity to talk about Jesus? I hope you feel like I do and sense an overwhelming feeling of joy and peace. Sharing Christ to others is not just good for them to hear and be ushered to the throne of grace, but it is also vital for us to share because it is an excellent reminder for us about who Jesus Christ is.

So, do we have to be the best or most convincing salespeople when we talk about Jesus? Not at all; but we should allow our passion for Him to come out in such a way that people are willing to listen. When we do not quench our love, the Holy Spirit uses that to draw people to God through Jesus Christ.

We will not always get our words correct; but we can continue to share the hope, joy, peace, love, grace the God through Jesus Christ offers the entire world.

JOURNAL TIME! How has the Holy Spirit worked in your life to shape the words you use in your daily interactions?

PEACE BEYOND UNDERSTANDING

Read Acts chapter 27

You know the feeling. You have had days where nothing seems to go right. Weeks. Months. Year(s). It is hard to see anything past what is going on right before us. We'll hear people say things like, just change your mindset and be more positive. But the truth is that is not what changes our mind, so we experience peace.

Paul, the prisoner who is part of the shipwreck, writes in Philippians 4:6-7 to be anxious about nothing, present your requests to God, you will experience a sense of peace beyond understanding (paraphrase). This same person wrote this when he was imprisoned earlier.

Imagine that. Peace in the midst of chaos. A sense of peace beyond understanding. Have you ever felt this before? This is more than a mere feeling. This peace is something that seems to overtake you and helps you be able to function in the midst of the chaos around you.

This is what I believe is happening to Paul. He is imprisoned, but he is on a voyage to Rome, and the ship he is on gets destroyed. He has to be the voice of reason and help the soldiers do the right thing because of faith not because of fear. We see what happens when people react from fear (soldiers) and also from faith (Paul).

So now the question remains, how do we get this kind of faith, this kind of peace? Paul did not do anything. Well, he did do one thing, he prayed and stayed connected to Jesus Christ. This kind of peace and discernment only came from God. God is the one who encouraged Paul and gave him the wisdom about what needed to be done to help protect and save the people he traveled with.

Peace is not the absence of conflict, but the presence of Christ. As you go about your day, your week, remember the only source of real peace comes straight from Jesus Christ. Keeping Jesus Christ at the forefront of your mind, of your heart, gives you the ability to remain outwardly and inwardly calm when everything else around you appears to be falling apart.

This is a great way to think about the Christian life of faith. It is through faith we believe God's presence is here and is real. It is through faith we believe the promises of God will stand firm and last eternally. It is through faith we believe we can do all that Christ calls us to. This faith is also a gift from God (Romans 12).

I invite you to take some time today and thank God for His presence. Seek him throughout your day because he is guiding you and is forming you to be a vessel to share his love and his grace. Everything around us does not have to be perfect, but we should remember we have a perfect God that is all around us and within us.

JOURNAL TIME! Tell of when you have felt a "peace beyond understanding" in your life.

THE JOURNEY CONTINUES

Read Acts chapter 28

P aul makes it to Rome.

His journey to Rome was full of turmoil, danger, unrest, and more. Yet through all of this, Paul kept his faith. That's remarkable!

Paul believed God when He said Paul would make it to Rome. I wonder how many times Paul had to remind himself of that? After all, the shipwreck would have been enough for many to give up and lose hope. But Paul does not lose his faith. He keeps encouraging the soldiers to keep going. He keeps sharing about God every chance he gets. Paul is the one person who seems to be holding it all together.

Think about your life journey. How many hardships have you lived through? How many times did you consider giving up? It would be the simple thing to do when things just got too hard for us; but we should keep pressing forward, especially if God has indeed called us to do what we're doing.

It would be so nice to be able to say that our life is going to be easy. But that would not be accurate. Our life will be filled with more hope, more peace, more joy, more love all because of Jesus Christ. Oh, we will falter at times; but He is always with us. Jesus guides us, and we get to bring people to Him in every circumstance.

What I love about the book of Acts is the movement of the Holy Spirit in the lives of ordinary people. Ordinary people who have answered the call of God on their lives and went out to do incredible things because of the power of the Holy Spirit within them.

Paul's life is remarkable, to me, because he seems to keep his faith (most of the time) in all situations. His is a story that inspires me, not to be just like Paul but to be able to continue proclaiming Jesus Christ wherever I am and through whatever I'm doing.

This may be the end of the book of Acts, but the story is not complete. We get to carry on what the Holy Spirit began in us. We get to continue spreading the good news of Jesus Christ to the ends of the world. How will you live out the calling God has placed on your life?

Acts 1:8 CEB
Rather, you will receive power when the Holy Spirit has come upon you, and you will be my witnesses in Jerusalem, in all Judea and Samaria, and to the end of the earth."

Matthew 28:19-20 CEB
Therefore, go and make disciples of all nations,
baptizing them in the name of the Father and of the Son
and of the Holy Spirit, teaching them to obey everything
that I've commanded you. Look, I myself will be with you
every day until the end of this present age."

JOURNAL TIME! God is using you to spread the Kingdom of Heaven wherever you go. What are you going to do about this task?

IT'S NOT OVER

This book was written as a series of daily devotionals over the course of a year. When we read through the Book of Acts, we can see the movement of the Holy Spirit doing incredible things in and through the early church.

I pray you have experienced an awakening of the Holy Spirit within your life and you live your life in such a way that you will witness "breakthroughs" in people's lives because of the incredible power of the Holy Spirit working within and through you.

I pray for you and would love to know how I can keep you in prayer (www.revryanstratton.com).

I leave you with these words from the Book of Jude:

To the one who is able to protect you from falling, and to present you blameless and rejoicing before his glorious presence, to the only God our savior, through Jesus Christ our Lord, belong glory, majesty, power, and authority, before all time, now and forever. Amen. (Jude 1:24-25 CEB)

ABOUT THE AUTHOR

Ryan Stratton is a local pastor in the United Methodist Church in Texas.

For over twenty years, Ryan has been teaching children, teenagers, and adults. While he was a teenager, he practiced TaeKwonDo and continued practicing and teaching the art form for fifteen years. While managing and owning his own schools he learned leadership, listening, marketing, and many other skills in order to be successful. After receiving a call to Christian ministry and leadership, Ryan is now in full time vocational ministry. Ryan's priority in life is to help people see and experience life beyond themselves and the purpose God has for them.

The most important relationships for Ryan are with his wife and his children. When not leading the church, studying the Scripture, speaking, writing (www.ryanstratton.com), or participating in community missions and outreach, Ryan is found spending time with his family while traveling, hiking, playing games, watching his kids play baseball and softball, and spending time with his wife.

Made in the USA
Lexington, KY
20 August 2018